AMY YOUNG

BECOMING MORE FRUITFUL

IN CROSS-CULTURAL WORK

HOW TO BE FREE IN CHRIST AND ROOTED IN REALITY AS YOU FULFILL YOUR CALL

Becoming More Fruitful in Cross-Cultural Work:
How to Be Free in Christ and Rooted in Reality as you Fulfill Your Call
By Amy Young

Published by Messy Middle Press

© 2022 Amy Young

Edited by Deb Hall of The Write Insight, www.TheWriteInsight.com.
Design by Vanessa Mendozzi

ISBN ebook: 979-8-9865482-1-0
ISBN paperback: 979-8-9865482-0-3

For my sisters, Elizabeth and Laura.

I love you.

CONTENTS

INTRODUCTION

I first encountered Maslow's hierarchy of needs in Mrs. Gunther's high school sociology class. As a brief reminder, the hierarchy can be visualized like a pyramid. At the bottom of the pyramid are the most basic and broad needs shared by all people and are classified as *physiological* needs. If those needs are met, you can move up the pyramid to the next level, which involves feeling safe and secure. Case in point, just this very moment, I paused to enjoy the fall leaves out my window because I feel safe, and safety is only possible because though my stomach might be telling me to get a snack, the truth is I'm well fed and had a decent night of sleep last night. As we move up the pyramid, after safety comes love and belonging; love and belonging are followed by self-esteem, and at the top of the pyramid is self-actualization. This is the embarrassing truth of what I remember most vividly of Maslow and his pyramid: Mrs. Gunther explained that being self-actualized is very rare. I don't remember the exact statistic, but 1 percent comes to mind—only about 1 percent of the population is able to self-actualize. Most people get no higher than having a healthy self-esteem.

My visceral reaction to this was part "Game on," part "Good, a way to show how special I am," and part "This is stupid. If something isn't attainable by all, the jig is rigged from the beginning." Ah, competitive nature combined with arrogance and a dash of social justice, meet the youthful me.

I hadn't thought about Maslow and his hierarchy in years until I wrote *Getting Started: Making the Most of Your First Year in Cross-Cultural Service*. One of the chapters discussed how a cross-cultural worker's relationship with God is different the first year on the field than it is in one's home country. In the chapter, I also wanted to find a way for the reader to connect with God during his or her first year in cross-cultural service, not simply point out a pitfall. The fruit of the Spirit mentioned by Paul in his letter to the Galatians seemed ideal. Returning to a familiar text when in transition could be the perfect way to move from the theoretical (bear fruit) to the practical (what it means to be loving) when adjusting to a new setting. For the first nine months, I encouraged the reader to focus on one fruit a month.

If you've lived abroad, I imagine you'd agree with me when I say, what could be more foundational than fostering love in the first month on the field? In my case, it meant a newfound "love" for sharing a home with rats and finding out my apartment's hot water pipes were broken and I would need to bathe at my teammate's apartment. I bet you have your own version of "Oh, okay, so this is real life and not the fantasy I imagined." But if you did the foundational work of fostering love for your new home, love for your new teammates and coworkers, love for your new culture, love for, well, just about everything, it made a difference, didn't it?

Then I moved on in month two to the next fruit: joy.

Ah, yes! The second month might be when joy starts to wane as all that's shiny and new can become less shiny, less new. As I wrote about love, and then joy, and then peace, and then patience, I began to notice how very pyramid-like they were as they built upon one another. Could it be that the fruit of the spirit were not merely a list but a hierarchy? I was curious, but I was also on a deadline and under a word constraint. I repeatedly told myself to stay focused and, no matter how interesting a rabbit trail was, to hop right on by.

And then tragedy struck. At least tragedy for this author. The manuscript was too long and six thousand beautifully placed words needed to be cut from the book. I am awful, awful, awful at conciseness. See what I mean? But six thousand words were doomed to be chopped.

What you hold in your hands started off as a three-thousand-word chapter called "God and You" in *Getting Started*. On that "chopping" day, as I read over the passage, I thought of how often those of us in cross-cultural work associate "bearing fruit" with the outcomes of our ministries. Teach in China (TIC), the organization I served with for nearly twenty years, had us fill out forms each semester trying to quantify the number of significant conversations, events, conversions, and discipleship activities we participated in. To be fair, I was also asked about my spiritual life. Years later, sitting in a cubicle in the quiet area of the library chopping away on the manuscript, I wondered, *What if the fruit of the Spirit was a focus for all cross-cultural workers and not just those in their first year? What if we switched the order and instead of talking about bearing fruit in our ministries, we talked about bearing fruit in ourselves? What if we trusted that the fulfilling of our calling was an outflowing of what God was doing in us? What if I chop these three thousand words from the manuscript, finish what I'm doing, and return to this later?*

So I chopped and moved on.

WHAT TO KEEP AND WHAT TO DISCARD

Paul's letter to the Galatians is one of the first letters he wrote. It's a front row seat to discussions and choices that are familiar to cross-cultural workers the world over. The church was young and trying to figure out what it meant to be a follower of the Way. Could Jews who now believed that Jesus was the Messiah now eat pork? Did they still have to practice circumcision? They wrestled with what *must* be kept, what could be left to personal choice to keep or discard, and what *had* to go in the new freedom they had. As a Christian American living in China, I faced similar choices. During a marriage ceremony, could a couple bow down to pictures of their ancestors, offering incense? I had friends who served in areas where Tibetan Buddhism faced even more complex questions because religion and culture are so entwined. All this to say, the Galatians weren't the only ones wading in these waters.

Shock, shock, what was considered essential and nonnegotiable was not as obvious as it might appear. (Apparently, sarcasm hasn't been discarded in my life in Christ.) At first I was surprised that some of my greatest culture stress came from working with someone from a different region of America who held different views on what men and women can do . . . and we're not even talking about what they can do in the church! *What do you mean, picking up a chair is men's work? Your arms look just fine to me,* I thought on more than one occasion.

Our worship services looked more like something from the early church than the larger, more organized churches my teammates and other foreign believers came from. Could we observe communion? Who could serve it? These discussions of what was essential for us and what we could do as "the church" sometimes became as murky and emotionally charged as anything out of the early church when Jews and gentiles first gathered together.

In his letter to the Galatians, Paul defends his authority and reminds the recipients of the true gospel (chapters 1–2). He then explains that because of what Christ has done, the law—which was good but always meant to be temporary—was no longer binding (chapters 3–4). At the beginning of chapter 5, Paul declares, "It is for freedom that Christ has set us free. Stand firm, then, and do not let yourselves be burdened again by a yoke of slavery" (Galatians 5:1). You can hear Paul's exasperation, and his flair for the dramatic, as he builds his argument using phrases like, "Mark my words!" (v. 2), "Who cut in on you to keep you from obeying the truth?" (v. 7), and my personal fave, "As for those agitators, I wish they would go the whole way and emasculate themselves" (v. 12). Ouch!

He wants them—former Jews and gentiles, fellow followers of the Way—to truly grasp the freedom they now possess and to understand that with great privilege comes equally great responsibility. Their freedom is not a free pass to sin; instead, their freedom should be used to love.

Anticipating their pushback and the loopholes they'd look for, Paul builds a case regarding the life of the flesh versus the life of the Spirit. Now things start to get linguistically interesting! Paul combines grammar and logic to make his point. He starts off by stating what should be apparent to all Galatians: you either walk by the Spirit or by the flesh. You cannot walk with one foot living according to the flesh and the other according to the Spirit.

Someone raised her hand and asked, "But, Paul, how can I know if I am walking by the spirit?" Okay, this is the Amy interpretation of the scene Paul envisioned as he wrote to them. But it is a fair question. In typical Paul fashion, he doesn't mince words; instead of softening the impact or offering them loopholes, he simply says, "The acts of the flesh are obvious" (Galatians 5:19). The acts of the flesh fall into four categories, and like the law, you only have to have one of them to be guilty of acts of the flesh. Here are the four categories from verses 19–21 in Galatians 5:

Sexual sins—"sexual immorality, impurity and debauchery"
Religious or spiritual sins—"idolatry and witchcraft" (sometimes translated as sorcery)
Social sins—"hatred, discord, jealousy, fits of rage, selfish ambition, dissensions, factions and envy"
Sins of the appetite—"drunkenness, orgies [sometimes translated as carousing], and the like"

Because some of these words might not be commonly used today, it's easy to gloss over them or give ourselves a pass. Dictonary.com defines debaucheries as "Indulgence in sensual pleasures; scandalous activities involving sex, alcohol, or drugs without inhibition."[1] Paul puts sexual immorality on the same playing field as impurity and debauchery. Even as I type this, I'm beginning to wonder what exactly qualifies as "indulgence." What exactly is "indulgence in sensual pleasures"? I just might be making Paul's point. The works of the flesh look for loopholes, missing the point of the freedom we have.

Whether we're a Galatian or a cross-cultural worker, as humans we are familiar with these four categories. Sexual sins happen. Paul's second category, spiritual sins, might look to many cross-cultural workers more like spiritual manipulation or abuse than bowing to an idol or participating in witchcraft. But let's not kid ourselves that our organizations and teams have never experienced spiritual sins. Continuing down the list, social sins may be our specialty on either end of the spectrum from socially strange to super goody-goody. If you grew up in the church, you probably learned to "socially appropriately" hate, which means you learned to clean up your hate so it didn't look like hate, but that doesn't make it less sinful.

The final category for works of the flesh involves sins of the appetite, probably the second most engaged in by the average cross-cultural worker. Since carousing sounds like something from a *Little House on the Prairie* episode or only something college kids do, you might think you get a pass. However, "and the like" looks like too much time on social media or video-streaming services watching movies and TV—all forms of self-soothing taken to a sinful degree.

By God's mercy, maybe debauchery or carousing isn't your vice, but I'm sure you've tasted jealousy or factions or envy. Bottom line, the acts of the flesh are about *all* areas of your life and Paul is not messing around when he concludes, "I warn you, as I did before, that those who live like this will not inherit the kingdom of God" (Galatians 5:21).

WHAT A DIFFERENCE AN *S* MAKES

Before we turn to the fruit of the Spirit, let's take a short grammatical detour. Paul could have said the "act of the flesh," but he used a plural form—acts—to show that works of the flesh can come in many forms. You don't need to do all of them to be defined by the flesh instead of the Spirit. In other letters Paul talks about gifts of the Spirit that help the body of Christ (1 Corinthians 12, Ephesians 4, and Romans 4). Gifts like discernment, healing, prophecy, and mercy are not given to every believer, but are sprinkled throughout the body; ideally, we rely on each other without becoming too isolated and independent from the body of Christ. In talking about *gifts* and *works*, Paul intentionally uses the plural form to show that no one will have *all* the virtues (gifts) or *all* the fleshy acts (works). The power and beauty of the gifts is that they show our mutuality and our need for each other. The acts of the flesh show our equality before the cross of Christ because, let's face it, even if we've been Christians for years, we all still sin.

Returning to the fruit of the Spirit and the freedom we have in Christ, Paul wants us to grasp how rich life in the Spirit is. "But the fruit of the Spirit is love, joy, peace, patience, kindness, goodness, faithfulness, gentleness, self-control; against such things there is no law." (Galatians 5:22–23 ESV). Notice the singular form *fruit*, not the plural, that he used for desires or gifts. Why the singular, Paul? In short, and please pay attention if you notice that your mind is thinking about dinner or an email you need to reply to: you can have *all* of the fruit. In my studies, when I began to grasp this basic truth, my mind was blown. It's not like you get patience, I get joy, and Bob gets self-control. Paul is showing that while the gifts and acts of the flesh are like a bowl of fruit, the fruit of the Spirit is like a bunch of grapes. One bunch made up of individual grapes. One person made up of nine attributes that can all exist at the same time.

Let me repeat, you can have all nine fruit of the Spirit at the same time.

This is the freedom Paul knows is possible for you and me and every believer who has ever existed in every culture. If the gifts show your mutuality and need for others, the fruit show your sufficiency and completeness. I will tip my hand and tell you the end of the book here at the beginning: because of the Holy Spirit at work in you, you already have all you need for an abundant life. Yes, you playing your part in the Great Commission is important, but it's not what ultimately defines you, nor is it the measure of what a fruitful life looks like. Let's reclaim our birthright from Eden and see that fruitfulness in ministry and life on the field starts inside us. While it is also responsible and wise to measure the fruit of your labors and the work of God with numbers and charts, those statistics are not the true measure of you as a laborer for Christ. When you or I elevate those types of "fruitfulness" above the fruit of the Spirit, we are walking by the works of the flesh.

As I've worked on this book and gotten to speak about this topic, I can't help but get excited when I talk about the freedom that God has for us. My voice goes up, my speed picks up the pace, and I start waving my arms. Beloved brothers and sisters reading this chapter, hear Paul afresh when he says, "Against such things there is no law!" (Amy-added exclamation point!). Christ died for your freedom from sin, and you have the Holy Spirit in you. It doesn't mean that life isn't still crappy and hard and injustice isn't real, but it does mean that even in the midst of the unbearably disappointing and confusing stuff of life, freedom exists too. Just as I did during my research, hear this afresh as well: the freedom that Paul never wearied proclaiming is for you too.

NOT A PYRAMID SCHEME

Remember how I wondered if the fruit of the Spirit are similar to Maslow's hierarchy with love being foundational and self-control being at the top? I'm not the only one to wonder about the order that Paul gives the fruit. The first three—love, joy, and peace—"appear to comprise Christian habits of the mind,"[2] and their primary direction is God-ward. The second three—patience, kindness, and goodness—are social virtues that primarily focus on the Christian in his or her relationship to others. The last three—faithfulness, gentleness, and self-control—concern the Christian as "he [or she] is to be in himself [or herself]."[3]

You might be familiar with the acronym JOY that helps priorities to be ordered on Jesus, Others, and You. The grouping of the fruit is similar: upward toward God, outward toward our fellow humans, and inward toward ourselves. Because I'm the master of shoving as many metaphors in one paragraph, I picture God as a kind juggling coach. Starting off with you tossing one ball from hand to hand, He throws in another, and another, helping you know how to relate to God, how to relate to others, and how to relate to yourself. All are a focus, all are of value, all need to be in play.

The very idea of fruit suggests that these virtues are the outflowing of the indwelling of the Spirit of God. A blueberry does not have to work hard to be round or sweet or blue. A watermelon does not have to hope it is juicy enough. So why does a book like this stir some of us up? Why does developing the fruit of Spirit feel more like the yoke of slavery with hidden messages than the abundant life? As you've been reading, the message you've heard could be, "You need to be more loving. You need to be kinder." Like the Galatians, our thinking about what freedom actually is has been tainted. Yes, you and I do need to keep growing in our ability to love, but not because we *should* be loving, which reeks with the death stench of the law, but because as we grow in love, we are freer and freer than we have ever been. It is for freedom's sake that we have been set free.

Before we move on to the specific fruit—fruits? Paul, what have you done to grammar— I want to acknowledge the limitation of any metaphor. For instance, the juggling metaphor a couple of paragraphs ago. While it's helpful to picture yourself able to have all of the fruit in your life as you keep the nine balls flying around you, the truth is we have all had times of greater or lesser love. We've all watched our patience dissolve before our very eyes. While a juggler works with static objects, even if they are juggling knives or sticks on fire, once they learn how to handle what they are juggling, the items don't change. Not so the fruit of the Spirit, which are dynamic. Love in your first year on the field will look different than love in your twenty-third year on the field. The good news is that you can grow in the fruit; the bad news is that you sometimes also shrink.

Even the concept of fruit, though extremely helpful, has limitations too. As true as it is that a blueberry doesn't need to work on being round or blue, it just is round and blue, you are not a blueberry. You can and do need to work on being kind or work on building your self-control muscles. An apple has no choice but to be an apple, but you do have some choice in the type of fruit you bear. You are part field, part farmer, part plant. In His paradoxical way, God works on you, outside of you, and through you.

As the field, your heart, thoughts, reactions, and responses can exhibit both the works of the flesh and the fruit of the Spirit. It is *you* who is being worked, even though it's true that the old is gone and, as the verse says, behold, the new is come, you are also in the already/not-yet dance. You are *already* a new creation in Christ, *and* you're *not yet* your perfected self.

As the farmer, you work the field and tend the plant. The farmer does as much as he or she can to create a conducive context. She plants in season. He waters faithfully. She checks for weeds and insects. He might even talk to his plants. But every farmer or gardener knows that much is out of his or her control. Without fail, every spring after our bleeding-heart plant is blossoming—which only lasts a few weeks out of the year—and the peony plant is weighed heavy with growing buds, we get a wet, heavy spring snow. Even though I fuss and fret and hate the damage the snow may bring, I still do my best to cover them before the storm. I love my plants and want to see the flowers bloom to their fullest, but every spring I have to accept the reality of forces outside my control.

As the plant, you bear the fruit. It's you who will experience the evidence of a bit more goodness, a bit more love, a bit more patience poking out of the soil that is your life.

You are the field, you are the farmer, and you are the plant. But in the end, I come back to the simple metaphor that Paul used: fruit. As a follower of Jesus and because the Holy Spirit is in you, you can bear much fruit. What if it *is* possible to be like a bunch of grapes and have love, joy, peace, patience, kindness, goodness, faithfulness, gentleness, and self-control at the same time? Paul longed for the Galatians to have the abundant life that Christ gives. He didn't want them, or you, or me to bear fruit because it is "the right thing to do." He wants us to bear fruit that is a result of choosing life over death, freedom over slavery, enjoyment over duty.

Paul didn't ask the Galatians to try harder, which would have been the law anyway. Instead he said, "So I say, walk by the Spirit, and you will not gratify the desires of the flesh" (Galatians 5:16). Walk. Not run, not even jog. But walk. Foot placed in front of foot. When the visa paperwork is taking forever or the electricity is out. When the twins of your local friend were born too early and the medical care is poor, or when you missed your family gathering . . . again. When the sun is shining and the church is growing and your children are thriving. Walk by the Spirit.

WHERE THE JOURNEY WILL TAKE US

For the last year freedom and fruitfulness have been my companions. You might say they have walked with me. Why is burnout on the field talked about so much? In part because it occurs too often, and partially because we emphasize ministry fruitfulness over personal fruitfulness, not realizing that one flows out of the other, while the other leads to death of a thousand cuts. Might I humbly propose we talk about burnout so much because we have gotten it wrong for so long that we don't even notice how off we are?

In talking about the works of the flesh, Paul said, "But if you are led by the Spirit, you are not under the law" (Galatians 5:18). I like how Eugene Peterson translated it from the Greek in The Message, as "the erratic compulsions of a law-dominated existence." Take a fresh look at these "erratic compulsions," as Paul lists them in Galatians 5:19–21, and see which ones you might have experienced recently:

- Repetitive, loveless, cheap sex;
- A stinking accumulation of mental and emotional garbage;
- Frenzied and joyless grabs for happiness;
- Trinket gods;
- Magic-show religion;
- Paranoid loneliness;
- Cutthroat competition;
- All-consuming-yet-never-satisfied wants;
- A brutal temper;
- An impotence to love or be loved;
- Divided homes and divided lives;
- Small-minded and lopsided pursuits;
- The vicious habit of depersonalizing everyone into a rival;

- Uncontrolled and uncontrollable addictions;
- Ugly parodies of community.

"I could go on," Paul concluded (Galatians 5:21 MSG). As I review the list, it overlaps with a report I read this very morning as to why people leave the field. Thankfully, the number one reason for leaving was completion of a term. This is good news! However, it was the avoidable reasons for leaving the field that saddened me, reasons such as conflict on the team, scandal, lack of role clarity, work/life balance, concerns over the integrity of teammates, and women being given fewer opportunities to contribute than men.[4]

God wouldn't tease us with freedom if it weren't possible. But what does freedom look like in the midst of the messy brokenness of this world? Once again, Peterson's translation in The Message helps me see the fruit of the Spirit from a different perspective than the familiar phrases and translations I grew up with. This is the freedom and the fruit Paul spoke of, "things like" these:

- Affection for others
- Exuberance about life
- Serenity
- A willingness to stick with things
- A sense of compassion in the heart
- A conviction that a basic holiness permeates things and people
- Involved in loyal commitments
- Not needing to force our way in life
- Able to marshal and direct our energies wisely. (Galatians 5:22–23 MSG)

Ah yes, that does sound like freedom. Even as I write this chapter, I can see that God needs to keep working in me because I approach the fruit like the gifts. I'm better at some than others. As I look over the above list and pair them with different personality tests, I can see how easy it is to think, "Oh, this type will be good at loyalty." Or "That personality will be good at directing her energies." It's not that this type of thinking is wrong; I'm just not sure it is very helpful when it comes to growth and walking with the Spirit. Instead, my hope is that the Holy Spirit uses these words and the time you spend reading and reflecting to transform you. We join the Galatians in needing to be reminded that "Since we live by the Spirit, let us keep in step with the Spirit" (Galatians 5:25).

• • •

The structure of this book follows the order Paul gave to the Galatians. The challenge for a book like this is that we can only discuss one fruit at a time, yet we're invited to experience them simultaneously. For me as a writer and you as a reader, I would like to solve this problem, but I can't. Instead, this is a tension we both need to manage. So, we will.

The first section of the book looks upward with chapters on love, joy, and peace. The second section looks outward at our relationships with others as we talk about patience, kindness, and goodness. The third section turns inward as we explore faithfulness, gentleness, and self-control.

This morning, as my spiritual director asked how she could be praying for me this month, I said that I need patience with God's pace and that I would be working on this book. "I want to marinate my soul in the fruit of the Spirit," I told her. As we ended in prayer, she reminded me of drinks at a fancy place that puts fruit in the water and the water becomes slightly flavored. Though it's a simple touch, it seems fancy. That is my hope and prayer for you: that you will sit with Jesus sipping fruit infused water—in other words, spend time with Him as He seeks to refresh you with water that goes a bit beyond plain water. And like that water, you and I will be infused by the fruit of the Spirit. I'll remind us every so often that though we are picking up each fruit and examining it separately, we can experience and be flavored by all of them at the same time.

UPWARD

LOVE

JOY

PEACE

LOVE

But the greatest of these is love.
—1 Corinthians 13:13

No matter what culture you come from, the idea of love has been shaped to some extent by the Hallmark Channel, sports stories, and Hollywood. In the end, the boy gets the girl, the team triumphs, and love hands out good feelings for everyone. Love might cost, but the cost is almost never greater than the rewards and love is often reduced to a mushy emotion. Don't get me wrong, the flooding of the brain with oxytocin feels good and is a gift from God! When little arms throw themselves around your neck, or that special someone catches your eye across the room, or you finally, finally, finally catch a glimpse of your loved ones coming through baggage claim having made it through customs, the oxytocin that is released strengthens bonds with people dear to you and feels so good.

That kind of love is easy to have flow from us. Who doesn't love love and connection and joy and knowing and being known? God gave it to us as a good gift, and we receive it as such. My point is not, "Down with all the good feelings!" Yet I sense, even within myself, the incompleteness this view of love offers. Here is why it is problematic: this view makes feelings the destination of love, instead of feelings being part of the journey. While feelings are one of the beautiful ways we are made in God's image, to limit love to "good feelings" is to cheapen the depth of this foundational fruit. Before we get to the Bible, let's take a brief tour though what has influenced our understanding of love.

In his well-known book on love, *The Four Loves*, C.S. Lewis examines four varieties of human love from Greek thought:

1. Familial or affectionate love (*storge*), the most basic form
2. Friendship (*philia*), the rarest and perhaps the most time consuming, the least celebrated, and the one we could live without
3. Romantic love (*eros*), passionate love
4. Charity or spiritual love (*agape*), the greatest and least selfish form of love[5]

One of the limitations of English is that unlike Greek, which uses four different words, we translate each of them as "love." I can say with equal truth and conviction, "I love this weather," "I love China," "I love my first grade teacher," "I love the Denver Broncos," "I love my nieces," and "I love creating material that helps cross-cultural workers." While it is true that I do love my first grade teacher, I have not seen her in decades. And I do love today's weather, but my feelings toward the weather are not like my feelings toward family members or good friends.

IS ABRAHAM WARM AND FUZZY?

Do you know the first time *love* is used in the Bible? Until working on this chapter, I didn't and was surprised that love did not appear until the twenty-second chapter with Abraham. Whoa, really? Abraham? Yup. There was no specific use of the word *love* surrounding creation. No use of the term between Adam and Eve or with their children. You might think Noah being mocked for working on the first ark in preparation for the near destruction of the whole world might have involved the mention of a little love. You would be wrong. Even though God blessed Noah in the first covenant of the Bible (the Noahic Covenant), and to this day we have rainbows as a sign of that covenant, the concept of love had not yet been mentioned in the Bible. After the flood and the covenant, generations were born and people began to spread out in the region. Next in the text come references to the Tower of Babel and the birthplace of thousands of languages. Despite the people's frustration inherent in not being able to communicate easily with other people, surely God expresses love for languages?! Still no mention of love; instead, we're told that God scattered people over the face of the whole earth (Genesis 11:9).

Abram enters the story in chapter 11 and is called in Genesis 12. But if you think that love is going to show up soon, hold your horses. We need to wait another ten chapters and journey to Egypt with Abram and Sarai. We also meet their nephew Lot and read about a bit of drama with him. God establishes His covenant with Abram. As the years pass and the covenant seems to be taking a lot longer than Abram thought it should, we have the attempted speeding up of the process with Hagar's pregnancy and birth of Ishmael. Then another covenant (this one of circumcision), a name change for Abraham and Sarah, and the three visitors who predict Isaac's birth. As if this wasn't all enough going on, Sodom and Gomorrah are destroyed. Abraham and Sarah move (again), and Abraham lies (again) to a leader about who Sarah is. God is gracious to Sarah and Isaac is born. Sarah is not gracious to Hagar, sending Hagar and Ishmael away. All of this without one word of love.

I go into such detail because it surprises me how many years passed, how many events happened, and how many people were mentioned before love was named. I'm not suggesting that God didn't love creation or humanity, but I am curious given how powerful naming was in the creation story, that love wasn't named earlier than it is. And I don't know about you, but when I think of Abraham, my mind does not instantly pull up "love." So, we have to ask why now? Why here? The first reference to love is a familiar story: "Then God said, 'Take your son, your only son, *whom you love*—Isaac—and go to the region of Moriah. Sacrifice him there as a burnt offering on a mountain I will show you'" (Genesis 22:2, emphasis mine).

Though this first reference seems a long time coming, this first use of *love* points forward to a day and time when another beloved Son would be offered as a sacrifice. John 3:16 is one of the most often quoted verses and one of the first taught to children and those young in their faith. "For God so loved the world that he gave his only Son, that whoever believes in him shall not perish but have eternal life." *God so loved the world.*

God is telling and showing us something about love. If the first use of love had been between a husband and wife, or even one between a parent and child that didn't involve potential child sacrifice, warm feelings might crowd out a greater truth about love. Love is more nuanced than warm feelings and may involve sacrifice. It might also involve vomit.

In early April of my second year in China I told my teammate I was going to take a nap after lunch because I wasn't feeling well. We both knew I must be sick because I am not a napper. Long story short, by late the next morning I started to vomit uncontrollably, and when Erin, my teammate, returned from teaching my class, she and two school officials took me to the local emergency room. I was hospitalized, and as the gurney was rolled outside onto the crowded street to go to another part of the hospital, I popped my contacts out and placed them in Erin's hand and slipped into a coma. Because I started experiencing seizures soon after that, the doctors weren't able to perform a spinal tap, and it was only confirmed later that I had bacterial meningitis. At that point it was assumed I would die. Erin's dad was a doctor, so she placed a long-distance call to him and described my symptoms. With a heavy sigh he told Erin he thought I had meningitis and even under the best of circumstances people died. In fact, a distant cousin of hers had recently died in America, and she needed to prepare herself that it was likely to be my fate as well. Though it was the middle of the night in America, he told Erin that my parents should be informed; he would call them to let them know what was happening.

Reflecting on it later, my dad said that phone call was one of the hardest calls Erin's dad ever had to make. In part her dad said, "I think the next call you will get is that Amy has died, and I thought you should know now." My parents called my sisters, who were stunned as well.

In one mercy after another, the hospital had the medicine I needed and I did not die. A British neurologist was working at the hospital and was able to talk to my parents, assuring them that while the conditions were not what they (or he) would want, the treatment I received was comparable to what I would've received in England or America. Since hospitals in Asia provided only medicine and medical care, not food or toilet paper, TIC flew a colleague to Chengdu to help Erin care for me. One of my first memories was several days after I came out of coma. Erin daily prepared and brought food for me. I can't remember exactly what she made, but it included oranges. Before I go on, you must know that Erin is one of the most lovely and refined people you will ever meet. Also remember that she had been on a tremendous roller coaster, and though I was alive, we still had a long haul in front of us. As I ate, we chatted with friends from our Sunday group who were visiting. Without warning, I sat up and projectile vomited all over Erin's sweater.

Mortified doesn't even begin to capture the horror I felt. *Did I just throw up on my teammate?!* Without missing a beat, this classy, refined teammate said, "It's no big deal," as she picked individual bits of orange off her sweater. Loving me cost Erin and others. My parents and sisters sacrificed by not coming to help, knowing their presence would divert from the help I needed because they couldn't function on their own in China. Erin's dad sacrificed by making a call to my parents when all he had was devastating news to deliver. Erin sacrificed again and again. Love that flows through you flows through sacrifice.

THROUGH SICKNESS AND IN HEALTH

Sickness and pain can show us who we are. Often our bodies tutor us in reality that we can apply to other areas of life. We meet the same grace in pain that we encounter in the quiet moments of the early morning, or on the beach, or in the hug of a child. But sometimes it seems that grace is a long way off and we don't feel loving. What then does love have to offer, in those moments when a situation isn't going to change because the illness is chronic, or our relative probably won't be freed from a mental illness this side of heaven, or the betrayal cuts so deep we think we'll die? In those moments we don't have to deny reality or try to find a way to ditch love.

At times I'd rather travel with revenge and hurt. I picture myself in a car with them on the road trip of life. We are cruising down a long stretch of open highway with nothing but time to kill, so I go over and over how poorly I feel, or what a nut a relative is, or fuss for the millionth time over the government's action or inaction. Revenge and hurt love these conversations and join in, bringing up details and points I had forgotten.

I forget that love is in the car. Every now and then love will try to interject into the conversation and raise her own point. Sometimes hurt or betrayal or disappointment will listen to love in the name of politeness and then get back to their point. Other times they scream at her, "You're naive! Have you forgotten . . . ," and then they recount a long list of wrongs. While this is one way to see my life, that car is on the path to slavery, not freedom. Walking with the Spirit doesn't ask anyone to get out of the car; instead, it rearranges who can sit where. Love is moved to the front seat with hurt, disappointment, and betrayal relegated to sharing the back seats. For many people, the idea that either love or hurt can be in the car, but not both, got introduced to the way they saw the world. But a car ride ignoring love or banishing hurt to the trunk is more like a ride at an amusement park. Any sense of actually going somewhere real is removed. Love is anchored in reality and always an advocate that there is room for all in the car as long as everyone knows where to sit.

When my nieces were young, they had assigned places in the car because of car seats or booster chairs. It was never a question of who would sit where. But as they each got old enough to experience the privilege of sitting in the front, politics entered the story. Though the customs and players are different, this sounds familiar, doesn't it? It's a current twist on the growth needed to move from being under the law to freedom. At first, rules such as circumstances, food laws, and guidelines for responding to circumstances were spelled out, but with freedom comes the messy discussion of "Can I eat this?" or, in my sister's car, "Where do I get to sit?" When it comes to our lives—yours and mine—freedom only works over the long haul if we let everyone in the car. Leaving disappointment or joy in the midst of heartache behind means that you won't be able to fully experience what it means to be human. It's when you can rant together over the annoying parts of your life and share the moments that are surreal that you are moving toward being integrated and more fully reflecting the image of God. Maturity comes when, in the midst of messy, confusing, and exhausting situations, love in the front seat is able to set the tone for the car and is not relegated to be squished in the back between annoyance and disappointment.

ANOTHER LOVE TEACHER

I find it confusing that our modern culture has relegated love to "that emotional stuff" and has mostly outsourced love to women. In many Western cultures, men are socialized to talk about love as long as it is directed toward their wife, kids, or a sports team. While you might not immediately think of Abraham when you think of love, you might remember that Paul wrote what is one of the most often quoted passage about love, 1 Corinthians 13. Paul: crusty, killer, convert, disciple of Christ . . . Paul. The passage about love being patient and kind is often used at weddings, and while weddings are an appropriate place to talk about love, Paul is getting at so much more! Just before he starts to wax poetic on love keeping no record of wrongs and always trusting in the good, he addresses a topic that tugs and pulls his listeners in different directions. Specifically, they are arguing over which spiritual gifts were the best gifts to have (see 1 Corinthians 12).

He's like a coach who calls a time-out in the middle of a crucial part in a game. You can picture the players huddling around Paul, catching their breath and listening intently.

Paul refocuses them as to how love *acts* and what love *does* for another. He reminds them (and us) that love needs to enter a story afresh because it has the ability to change the trajectory. English uses adjectives in 1 Corinthians 13 when the original Greek didn't use adjectives. Instead, the passage has been described as "maniacally verb-centered"; for instance, what is often translated as "is kind" in English is the verb "kinds" in Greek.[6] This direct translation from Greek to English helps me see the verbs in action (I've offset it because in the original Greek there was no punctuation and it can be hard to read):

> The love endures long acts kindly the love not acts jealously not acts brutally not boasts not gets full of itself not disgraces itself not seeks what is its own not gets irritated not reckons up the evil not rejoices in the injustice but rejoices together in the truth endures everything believes everything hopes everything endures everything the love never falls.[7]

Love "endures everything" is listed not once but twice. Paul was compelled to stress that no matter what, love endures. "Do you get it?" he seems to ask. "Keep on loving, even when it is tempting to quit." "Kinding" is hard and unrelentingly necessary.

I was talking with my colleague Dennis about an upcoming transition he was embarking on and the challenge it can be to end well. He pooh-poohed the suggestions I made. *Hello,* I thought, *I've written a book on ministry transitions and helped thousands navigate transitions that seem larger than the one you're going through. I know what I'm talking about.*

The very moment I am with another person, I have a choice: am I going to "kind" them or "unkind" them? This expression of love can only come with the help of the Spirit. So, sensing that Dennis wasn't interested in talking about it anymore, I switched subjects. In the weeks to come, he didn't finish particularly well. Publicly, it wasn't too bad, but behind the scenes he didn't leave detailed notes for others to follow in his footsteps. In a final team meeting where we all discussed details of his job to be sure we could continue on, he kept saying, "Oh yes, that's in the drive." Sometimes he'd say he'd "add that to the drive" and then type a line or two on his computer. As I look back on that scene, I can see the assumptions I made and wish that I had asked a few clarifying questions. Later that day, after turning in all of his keys and officially finishing his duties, Dennis emailed the rest of us a link to "the drive." Imagine my shock when it turned out to a two-page document. That is, one single document. Not plural. No series of documents covering all the programs and ministry details we had discussed. In addition, I found out that the week before, he'd told another teammate that I was the reason he was leaving . . . because, according to him, I had been secretive about a hiring process he'd been involved in for months.

The upside of being part of a team is that others were as surprised as I was to hear he resigned because of my "secretive-ness." It seemed that was his excuse to help assuage the discomfort he felt about leaving. After twelve years and several significant political and cultural shifts, it was a sad note on which to end our working relationship. In these instances, my immediate desire is for others to know that I have "been done wrong." Oh, the urge to "unkind" Dennis was strong! When I noticed that I wanted to be unkind to him, I had a choice: to walk in the flesh or with the Spirit. In those moments, my thoughts or feelings can rush ahead and encourage me to respond too quickly without allowing a pause. Part of walking with the Spirit means that you and I can have human responses to situations. We can feel the ire rising and acknowledge that, as in my situation with Dennis, a wrong truly has occurred.

But it also allows us to remember that a larger reality will live longer than the moment that is taking place. Love invites us to live a bigger and broader story. In this case, Dennis relocated and I continued to work with people who knew and loved him. In the months that followed, I was grateful that love helped me to "kind" him and his memory. When Paul was talking to the Corinthians, he was addressing real people in messy situations similar to the ones you and I face. Love is possible, not outside of these situations or in spite of them, but right smack dab in the middle of them.

Paul ends the "time-out" about love with the reminder that maturity requires us to put away childish behavior. "Now I know in part; then I shall know fully, even as I am fully known. And now these three remain: faith, hope and love. But the greatest of these is love" (1 Corinthians 13:12–13). You can almost hear him clap his hands and say, "The time-out is over, get back in the game," as he continues the discussion of gifts of the Spirit in 1 Corinthians 14. If he were writing to you, Paul might say, "Get back to loving your family, loving your host culture, loving your organization, loving many of the parts of being a cross-cultural worker. It's messy and hard, and you will be tempted to get off course by talking about who is better at what. The only way to do any of this cross-cultural life is with love."

Returning to Galatians, I don't want to miss the freedom that love offers. Paul adamantly insists that true freedom only exists by walking with the Spirit, not walking by our own strength. So, what is the choice that you and I make when we choose to walk with the Spirit? In this case, when we choose to love and to let the Holy Spirit help us love, we gain connection. Love is foundational because it provides the pathways of connection. Given the four types of love that Paul could have used—*storge, philia, eros,* or *agape*—he chose *agape,* the love of charity, connection, and sacrifice. You've probably heard the adage that we have freedom *for* something and freedom *from* something. If it truly is a freedom for connection, that means it is a freedom from something as well. Love frees us from isolation.

As part of the three fruit—love, joy, and peace—that orient us toward God, it's no surprise that love is first. Connection is one of the ways we are made in the image of God. God's very nature is rooted in the communion of the Father, Son, and Spirit. Unlike the trinity, where Father, Son, and Spirit experience ongoing mutual affection for each other, our love waxes and wanes when we try to love out of our own strength. Who are we kidding? Even with the Holy Spirit walking with us, this good gift needs to be guarded. In a counseling course, I was introduced to a simply model called TFA. It's drawn as an inverted V with "Thoughts" written on the left of the inverted V, "Feelings" at the top, and "Actions" on the right. Basically, our thoughts, feelings, and actions are related to one another, but often we don't see the relationship between thoughts and feelings. Feelings are more obvious to see when they play out in our actions. I might *feel* hurt, so my response to you (my *action*) is abrupt or limited to a one-word answer. But *feeling* hurt did not just happen; it came from a *thought.* Maybe I thought,

Well, I guess I'm not as important to the team as I thought. If I was, I would have been told about the meeting more than five minutes before it happened! This thought leads to me feeling hurt, which leads to my abrupt interactions as a result.

And since we are talking about agape, let me say, I appreciate God acknowledging that love both offers and costs us something as well. Thus, we need our thoughts and feelings to be more, shall we say, open in their communication with one another. Some people are going to be more aware of their feelings, so they may need to work backward and ask themselves, "What is the thought behind this?" Others might need to be more aware of their thoughts and use the language of "I think" more naturally. They may need to ask themselves, "What feeling or feelings could this thought lead to?" And for a very few people, they are not overly aware of either feelings or thoughts. If you're one of those people, start with what you know: What actions have you taken? Did you walk out of the room? Did you call a friend to vent? Did you clam up and stop interacting? Ask yourself about what you were thinking or feeling.

For all of us, this might feel a bit awkward and artificial at first because we're so used to the automatic ways we respond. With practice in situations that are easy to notice what's going on, we will become more able to understand more complex situations and respond to them in and with love. Over the years, I have had dozens of teammates, and though Erin is the only one I physically threw up on, they all had opportunities to love me and be loved by me. I'll share in the next section something my mom told me years ago that has helped me to love others well.

WHEN LOVE ISN'T EASY

Most evenings when my dad came home from work, he and mom would sit in the living room talking over their day while my sisters and I watched a sitcom rerun on TV. My dad was an engineer and a verbal processor; the combination meant he went into great detail about whatever project he was working on. One day I asked my mom if she actually enjoyed hearing all the details, because I found them unbelievably boring. (Oh, the unfiltered unkindness of youth.) Her answer stopped me in my arrogant tracks. "The *L* in love stands for listen. I love your dad, so I listen to him share."

When we walk with the Spirit, one of the ways we can love each other is simply to listen. We live in an era that loves (see what I did there?) big gestures. But staying love, day-in-and-day-out love often comes more quietly. I can buy into the lie that love is mostly a feeling that flourishes in ideal environments. Slowly, very slowly, the truth that I can experience the freedom of love at all times and in all circumstances is seeping in. This freedom helps me to look for other fruit of the Spirit. Love is foundational, but it's not alone. Slowly, very slowly, I am growing in believing that all nine fruit can coexist at the same time and support each other.

LET US PRAY

Drawing from the *Book of Common Prayer* and Galatians 5, we'll build this prayer at the end of each chapter, adding to it as we go:

Grant me, O Lord, for your sake, through the work of your Holy Spirit, love for those I've come to serve and those I serve with. Amen.

JOY

Rejoice in the Lord always. I will say it again: Rejoice!
—Philippians 4:4

The first memory I have of pure unadulterated joy on the field involved a basketball court and a bike. To help you picture it, I was in my mid- to late-twenties. I'm wired for optimism, adventure, and a tendency to downplay the harder parts of life. I can't say what I'm about to share was my first wave of joy in China, but I can say it is the memory that has stood the test of time. Members of the English Department at the campus where we taught were in a basketball tournament and asked my teammate Erin and me to be on their team. Since the department leaders had gone through the hassle of helping to procure our visas, and "all Americans are good at basketball," they might as well get the benefit of our assumed basketball abilities.

As it turns out, they were sadly wrong when it came to my ball skills. Alas. When they originally asked (told) us about the game, I was still in the "I'm trying to figure this culture out and I do not want to offend" phase, so I said yes to any request. Then, there I was, making it painfully obvious to everyone watching that the only thing I was quite skilled at is semiviolent fouling. Our fellow athletes were adult Chinese students who were about the size—and this truly is not an exaggeration—of my thigh if my thigh was about five feet tall. When I pictured myself serving in China, sharing the good news, willing to do anything for the cause of Christ, I have to admit that "play basketball" never ever occurred to me as one of the ways I'd serve God.

It was a crisp November late afternoon, and because few options for entertainment existed, the sidelines were packed. Honestly, the game wasn't *that* bad, but when everyone else on the court was so much better than I was, I wasn't enjoying myself. This was one of those moments when you whisper to yourself, "Smile and endure this; and please, please, Amy, rein in your elbows and their violent tendencies. You know, when you're frustrated and feel out of control, you are not at your best. Please do not do something you will live to regret!"

The game ended with a sigh of relief that my public humiliation was over. Erin and I chatted with a group of our students for a few minutes before we biked back to our apartments. "Robbie," as he was called in English class, asked an innocent question with a twinkle in his eye. A few months before, he'd spearheaded the small committee of students who took Erin and me to the used bicycle market to purchase bikes. On that September day, he made us stay out of the market so that we wouldn't be overcharged for our bikes. He'd unfolded a piece of newspaper, set it down, "because the bench was dirty," and firmly told us to keep a low profile while he bargained for the bikes. Robbie was one of those gems who helped us understand and adjust to Chinese culture.

Fast-forward to the basketball court, almost as an afterthought, before we all said good-bye and headed off for dinner, Robbie wondered if Erin and I had ever ridden double on our bikes. Though technically illegal to ride someone on the back of your bike, it was

34

a common practice. A bit of skill was required for both the person pedaling the bike and for the person sitting on the back rack.

"No, we've never ridden double." With his mischievous grin, he asked if we wanted to learn. Even though it looked fun, my immediate thought was, *No way can someone the size of my thigh safely bike with me on the back of their bike.* Since the court was mostly empty by that time, Erin and I threw caution to the wind and said, "Sure." We needed to learn how to do it and were far enough into life in China . . . why not now? While I do not remember how Robbie taught us to ride double, a string of pictures a student took on my camera shows the laughter and the joy. In one photo Erin is pedaling and I'm sitting sidesaddle on the back with my arms around her waist. She's leaning forward, laughing, and I have my head thrown back, laughing as well. When I think of joy, I think of that picture.

You know the kind of joy I'm talking about. The kind that is part in awe that *this*—whatever the *this* may be—is your life. Part awareness of how much you are enjoying the moment. And part holy humility as you sense what a gift a moment like this is from a heavenly Father who knows what makes you happy and gives good gifts. It's easy in this kind of joy to see the freedom that walking with the Holy Spirit can offer. These are the times it's easy to sing, laugh, even sigh over the truth that "the joy of the LORD is my strength" (Nehemiah 8:10). But not all of life is this way.

AFTER REALITY HITS

When I prepared to write this book, I planned to write through the fruit of the Spirit in the order they were presented. With the grouping of the fruit focusing upward, then outward, and finally inward, the plan to write in order provided a writing road map.

I finished the love chapter on a Friday afternoon. When the time came, the following bright Monday morning to write on joy, I didn't want to write about joy. I was ten days into an ankle injury that had me only semimobile. I'd tripped on dry grass. Not only was I injured, I'd been denied a good story. The ten days prior had reminded me that my mental health was tied to physical activity. So, what does joy look like when what makes you joyful is taken away (or at least benched for a season)?

Add to that, I sound whiny and ungrateful. You might be rolling your eyes at me right now and listing off what you're facing. Even if your life is fairly smooth, we both know that all kinds of natural disasters, political unrest, systemic injustice, human trafficking, addictions, abuse, and dysfunction exist around the world. Is joy an appropriate response to the hardships of life, whether relatively small (like my ankle injury) or large (like any of those listed in the previous sentence)? Does God want us to fake it until we make it?

I am comforted that the fruit of joy is listed early, showing that, like love, it's foundational to who we are, and not tagged on as something "good Christians should do or feel." Joy is one of the hallmarks of Christians because it is one of the hallmarks of God. Many hours of my childhood were spent on the road between Colorado and Michigan making cross-country trips to visit my grandparents. Because this was in the days before cell phones, Grandma and Grandpa would roughly know the time that we hoped to arrive. They waited for us in the screened-off porch, watching the driveway. One of the fondest sounds of my childhood was my grandpa's laughter. He loved peanuts, so we brought him a jar of peanuts whenever we visited. Nothing special, just regular peanuts from the grocery store. But his chuckle of delight as we gave him his gift was a taste of God's delight in us. In an era that celebrates big gestures on social media, we need to guard our thinking about what brings joy to God and where God offers ordinary joy.

This fruit can be an easy casualty of dichotomist thinking to circumstances. *I'll be joyful when* can slip into our under-explored thoughts, assumptions, and hopes. *When I get married, when the support is all raised, when the winter ends . . . then I will* be happy, relieved, or able to really enjoy life. The truth is, getting married will bring joy, seeing support comes in does bring joy, and the long cold days of being trapped inside are hard. Experiencing joy doesn't mean that we have to stop having authentic responses and become a plastic version of a person. Years ago, in an adult Sunday School class I taught, an elderly lady, said, "I never become angry." I pushed her a little bit, but because it was a public space and it became abundantly clear she was not going to budge from her statement, I let it go. She was proud that she never got angry because "good Christians" don't get angry. (I don't know what she would make of Jesus clearing the temple.)

God does not want you to choose between a false joy—one that can't handle emotions like anger—or having no joy. Instead He invites us to an integrated life. A life of joy *and* whatever other emotions you may have. Sometimes joy will come easy, like joy *and* singing, but other times it will be joy *and* weeping. Part of walking with the Spirit is learning to experience joy with the "ands" of life.

JOY AND SINGING

The used bike that Robbie helped me buy ended up being one of my most beloved possessions; I even named her Lucille. You know when you buy something used or secondhand but it seems practically new? This was not the case with Lucille. While she wasn't on her last legs, she was no spring chicken. Some of my earliest solo language experiences involved the kind bicycle repair men who knew far more about bikes than I did and understood my "point at the problem" approach to bicycle maintenance. Chengdu had wide, flat bicycle lanes that were great for biking when it wasn't rush hour. I felt like Maria Von Trapp from *The Sound of Music* as I biked around, so happy that I couldn't help singing songs about Lucille or my life in China. "It's a fine time to leave me, loose wheel," I'd belt out as I twisted Willy Nelson's lyrics to fit my China life.

I'm not alone when it comes to singing and joy. David's thankfulness often flowed out in joyful song after song in the Psalms:

But let all who take refuge in you be glad; let them ever *sing* for joy. Spread your protection over them, that those who love your name may rejoice in you. (Psalm 5:11)

Sing to him a new song; play skillfully, and shout for joy. (Psalm 33:3)

May the nations be glad and *sing* for joy, for you rule the peoples with equity and guide the nations of the earth. (Psalm 67:4)

They tell of the power of your awesome works—and I will proclaim your great deeds. They celebrate your abundant goodness and joyfully *sing* of your righteousness. (Psalm 145:6–7)

While the italics are mine, look back at the reasons for singing. God provides refuge, and when we stop and notice the areas of refuge in our lives, joy can bubble up. God rules with equity and His works are awesome. Though we may not always see the evidence of equity or awesomeness, we don't have to contort ourselves to force ourselves to see them. One of my seminary professors said that some Christians are too quick to play the "mystery card." They default to explaining confusing or seemingly contradictory occurrences by saying it's all part of God's mystery. On the flip side, others try to study or rationalize everything without leaving any room for God's mysterious ways. He encouraged us to do our due diligence and study a question or confusing passage and to leave room for God's mysterious ways too. Singing and joy doesn't mean you have to lie and force a song out of your heart, but when you notice God's righteousness, places He provide refuge, and even small areas where God's equity is breaking into a system, let joy be present in the messy middle and do not wait until the completed story.

Recently, one of my nieces asked me not to sing so much in public. She's a teenager and my songs about what I'm going to buy at the store or what I think of the weather are embarrassing; I get that. I hadn't realized I was singing that much. The irony is that instead of being known for my singing, I've written about dreading all of the singing in heaven. It's a bit embarrassing when the subject of heaven comes up and someone turns to me and say, "I know you don't really like singing for ten thousand years." Okay, so maybe I have made my dislike at the thought of singing for centuries known a bit too much. So, being asked not to sing by my niece caught my attention. I was singing nonsense songs about my life, and my niece's comment helped me see that silly songs are one of my "I'm in a good place" meters.

We all have an "I'm in a good place" meter when joy flows easily and is in sync with other parts of our lives. Yours might not be singing, but you have a tell, in other words, something about your behavior or demeanor that provides clues about the hand life's dealt you at the moment. I remember a three-month period where I felt like I was living in a Disney cartoon. I was aware I was in a joy bubble because life felt good, good, and very good. One day, as I walked the early morning Chengdu streets, I sensed God say, "It's not sustainable that life will always be this good, but it is now, so enjoy it!"

You can sing with joy because God first sang over you. The prophet Zephaniah writes that God will "take great delight in you; in his love he will no longer rebuke you, but will rejoice over you with singing" (Zephaniah 3:17). I love the picture of God signing His version of silly songs over me as an overflow of his delight. *Amy makes her beeeeed like a champ and then she brushes her teeeeeth and smiles like a cute caaaat. I loooooovvveee her! Next we'll have a cup of teeeeaaaa together and enjoy the morning! This is gonnaaaaaaa be a great day!*

God sings over you, too, you know. Take a moment and imagine the different sounds and rhythms used to create music in the different cultures you've lived in or visited. God loves music! While music and singing can be for times when joy easily flows through you, thankfully joy is not limited to those expressions.

JOY AND WEEPING

It's true that God delights over you and He's a father who gives good gifts, so it's no surprise to find joy amongst good gifts, am I right? Just think of the delight on a child when they open a present you've been counting down the days or hours for them to open because you know it will bring squeals of delight. But joy is yours in times of sorrow too. Before we get to the joy in sorrow, let's acknowledge the sorrow in sorrow. Jesus wept when his friend Lazarus died. He also wept over Jerusalem and the sinful actions toward the prophets. He allowed His followers to see that He was moved in His personal life by the death of a friend and on a broader scale for a city and system that had failed to do right. The psalmist often talked about tears of sadness on multiple occasions.

One of the challenges of being a Great Commission worker is that to a certain extent, your job is God. You've probably seen God show up in amazing ways and work in ways that include directly answered prayers, some of which could only be called miraculous. Yet you've also seen what seems to be the silence of God. Why wouldn't He heal that child? Provide for specific needs? Or grant that visa? When I had meningitis and nearly died, I romanticized my suffering when I was in the middle of it. While I was still in the Chinese hospital with meningitis, it was obvious I would live but not obvious how much brain damage I would have.

I assumed God was going to use my suffering in a revival. Why else would He have me go through awful pain, the humiliation of so many people seeing me in various stages of being undressed in the hospital, and the agonizing healing process of learning to walk, feed, and dress myself . . . but for something big, right? Can you see how quick I was in suffering to try to make meaning of my suffering? I was willing to suffer if it meant that my students and local friends came to Christ. But guess what? That didn't happen. Instead, my students attributed my healing to the fact that I was a foreigner and given special treatment. They were not wrong. After the shock wore off and I returned from a month of recuperating in Hong Kong, people were happy to see me, but they were not moved to thank God. Even though I returned to teaching part-time, it was clear I was not yet back to myself and had a long road of healing in front of me. I was confused at God's inability to "capitalize" on my suffering.

Psalm 42:2–3 (MSG) captures the confusion I felt:

I wonder, "Will I ever make it—
	arrive and drink in God's presence?"
I'm on a diet of tears—
	tears for breakfast, tears for supper.
All day long
	people knock at my door,
Pestering,
	"Where is this God of yours?"

You might be on a diet of tears and wondering how joy fits into your reality. You don't have to have joy because of your suffering, your tears are appropriate. God isn't a sadist delighting in pain. But He also doesn't see suffering as the finale of a story. Psalm 30:5 reminds us that "his anger lasts only a moment, but his favor lasts a lifetime; weeping may stay for the night, but rejoicing comes in the morning." When tears are the appropriate response to a situation, cry. It's also okay to be confused and to find safe places to ask the hard questions. God doesn't ask us to try to ignore confusion or pain.

Trying to hold hard questions down is like trying to keep a beach ball under water. You can for a while, but eventually the ball is going to pop up. Don't force a happy ending too soon or a tidy explanation of what God is up to in the suffering you or others around you experience. But also don't forsake the hope that God is at work and that it is possible to have tears *and* joy—if not on the same day, then at least in the same story. Another psalm—the Psalms are so good at creating space for a nuanced reality—says that when you "go out weeping," you "will return with songs of joy" (Psalm 126:5–6).

Joy may not be the first reaction to a situation, but thanks to the Holy Spirit being alive in us, it can be a quiet companion. Part of walking with the Spirit is to notice joy woven into hard situations. Sometimes joy is easy to name, like when I was able to shuffle down the hall to the public telephone and hear my parents' voices on the other end, knowing that I would live. Other times, it's not so easy to label something as "joy," and we need to look for the small places that we can rejoice. I could rejoice that groups of three students stayed with me each night so that Erin could go home and get some much-needed sleep. However, after the first night when they hovered over me all night long, I almost lost it and yelled, "Back off!" at them. We worked out a deal that they could "keep watch over me" by sitting in chairs along the wall. At that moment I couldn't see that the Holy Spirit was walking with me by controlling my tongue. Looking back, my joy is in the form of quiet rejoicing that I didn't yell at them when I wasn't my best. Lest I make myself sound holier than I am, I can confidently say it would have been a quiet joy even if I had yelled. The Holy Spirit walks with us and works even, perhaps especially, in those situations when we are not our best. The joy that can seep in after an apology, when we realize all is not lost, is not less joy. I'm slowly leaning into the truth that walking with the Holy Spirit means allowing the fruit a full range of expression.

ORDINARY JOY

I awoke one morning in Beijing to an email from my oldest niece, Emily, with the subject line "Math Fairy I Need You."

> Dear Math Fairy,
> I am in desperate need of your help! I wrote a poem about math to help you understand my feelings toward it. Hope you enjoy it :-(.
>
> **"What Math Is to Me"**
> By Emily
>
> Math is evil,
> Unforgiving.
> Math is hard to understand.
> Math is way worse than a first grade band.
> Math is hated,
> Unlegible,
> Math is hard for me.

• • •

Wow. I have never written a poem to express my feelings about anything without it being assigned. Clearly, she had strong feelings about math, so TMF (The Math Fairy) wrote the following response:

> Dear Emily,
> (This is Math speaking, by the way, I'm borrowing Aunt Amy's computer). I thought I'd start off with a poem about what you are to me.

"What Emily Is to Me"
By Math

Emily is kind.
Her smile warms me.
She helps people,
and her laugh is like listening to a cool summer brook.
She is loved.
I want her to be my friend.

• • •

Hey, what was Math doing on my computer? This is now Aunt Amy . . . looks like Math wrote something. Let me see what she said. (I'm back now, I scrolled up.) I agree with Math's poem about you! It seems that she knows you well even though it's a little hard for you to know her. Is that another way of seeing it? (She's not really evil, you know. Not like a wicked stepmother in Cinderella!)

I am seriously sorry that math is so frustrating for you. But know that Math wants you to "get" her. She's not playing hide-and-seek or being mean. She likes you. Not as much as I do! But she *does* like you.

And I LOVE you :)!

Love,
AA (Aunt Amy), aka The Math Fairy

Through this exchange, and the subsequent emails, I discovered that Emily had a poetry notebook and often wrote poems to process and express her life. That's right. Poetry. Sometimes joy can show up in an unexpected place on an ordinary day, like this insight into her life. As an aunt living far away from young nieces, her email delighted me. Of course, I was sorry that she was having such a rough go with math, but being a small part of her life through that email exchange reminded me that joy can show up in the simple act of checking my inbox.

Recently I noticed a verse I must've read multiple times. Hannah, the mother of Samuel, was only able to see him once a year when the family traveled to Shiloh to offer their annual sacrifice. While recording how wicked Eli's sons were—the NIV describes them as "scoundrels"—Samuel is reported as ministering before the Lord in his linen ephod, or apron. I wasn't surprised that Eli's sons were scoundrels or that Samuel was working with Eli and his sons. I knew that, but what I hadn't noticed was 1 Samuel 2:18–19: "Each year his mother made him a little robe and took it to him when she went up with her husband to offer the annual sacrifice." I can picture Hannah choosing the material, cutting it out, and sewing love into every stitch. I imagine the joy she took in this ordinary task, knowing it was what she *could do* for her child. And then I wonder about the anticipation building as she packed her bag and started the trek toward her son, knowing she would only see him for a short period. Eager to see how he had grown in a year. Loving him as much as her other children, even though their time in person was so limited. This nugget in 1 Samuel reminds us cross-cultural workers that joy span distances and seeps into ordinary moments in ordinary days.

Joy isn't just for the exciting, fun moments or for the sake of hope infused into times of suffering. It's also for the moments when you check email, wait for the bus, or learn something new about your host culture. Joy lives in the ordinary too.

WHAT ABOUT THE GALATIANS?

The Galatians weren't so different from us. Cross-cultural workers might not wrestle with whether or not Christians need to be circumcised, but we have our own issues that can pull teams or organizations apart. One year during annual meetings one of the workshops offered by my organization was titled "China's Changing. Are We?" In the early years in a culture, it can be easier to stay open to change because much of life is new. In this first grouping of fruit that is more upwardly focused—love, joy, and peace—joy is the oil that keeps a machine from rusting. Joy is for every phase of life on the field. In the early days you pinch yourself and squeal with joy, "I can't believe I'm here!" Or you're in shock over what your life is actually going to look like, and joy quietly sits beside love even if you can't see anything to rejoice over. It's also for those ordinary days when over the years the shine of the adjustment is gone and life has settled into a comfortable rhythm.

Whether in happy circumstances, sad ones, or merely on ordinary days, joy points to the bigger picture and plants one foot in the here and now and another in eternity.

Paul knew that like the Galatians, we need to be reminded of the freedom that is at stake. Left on our own, we can each be drawn to bondage of the law or to other activities that offer false hope to overcome the difficulties of life. If love offers us the gift of connection to each other, what does joy offer? When you walk with the Spirit, you can have what Peterson translated in The Message as "an exuberance about life." Just think, the fruit of joy protects you from despairing. It helps you avoid becoming jaded or despondent when injustice seems to hide behind every corner or weariness settles in.

Earlier we talked about how this first grouping of fruit can also be categorized as habits of the mind. As a habit of the mind, joy enters through the habit of gratitude. "Gratitude shifts you from the *lack* state and puts you in the *have* state."[8] In a letter from James to the scattered twelve tribes, he told them to "count it all joy" (James 1:2 ESV) or "consider it pure joy" (NIV) when we face trials. Why? "So that you may be mature and complete, not lacking anything" (James 1:4). Maturity is part of the freedom Paul longs for the Galatians—and you and me—to have. When I was a young child, we were allowed to answer the phone after some coaching from Mom. Even then, we knew that answering the phone was a privilege (oh, for those good ole days, am I right?!) that came with our growing maturity.

If the opposite of joy is despair, the presence of joy points to your growing maturity. During my studying and writing of this book, I've needed to return to the truth that all nine fruit can be at work in me at the same time, not just one at a time. Life on the field can be all of the areas we've touched on, be it pure joy like the kind I experienced in the bike story at the beginning of the chapter, or more nuanced situations that might involve loss or ordinariness. Because joy is a habit of the mind, be encouraged that nothing in your circumstances may change, but that doesn't mean you can't increase in the joy you experience. We have one more fruit in our upward category, one that rounds out these habits of the mind with a depth that only this fruit can bring.

LET US PRAY

Let's continue to build this prayer as we move forward through this book:

> Grant me, O Lord, for your sake, through the work of
> your Holy Spirit, love for those I've come to serve and
> those I serve with and joy in the midst of the mundane
> and the miraculous of my life. Amen.

PEACE

The LORD turn his face toward you and give you peace.
—Numbers 6:26

One of the first scriptures I memorized as a child was Psalm 23 (KJV): "The Lord is my shepherd. I shall not want. He maketh me to lie down in green pastures: he leadeth me beside the still waters. He restoreth my soul: he leadeth me in the paths of righteousness for his name's sake. Yea, though I walk through the valley of the shadow of death, I will fear no evil: for thou art with me; thy rod and thy staff they comfort me." As a child I didn't know about translations—this is the King James Version—or old English or that the Bible could change. (Okay, okay, friend. I don't mean that the Bible changes; I mean that languages change and we no longer say "maketh," "restoreth," or "leadeth," unless you are an American thinking that's how proper Brits sound.)

To this day, reciting Psalm 23 evokes peace, and as I say it aloud, inhaling and exhaling slowly, I can feel my heart rate calm. If I'm not aware, I can let my mind wander to a place that is outside of the actual psalm and more a place of fantasy. In my mind's eye, the green pastures that God has me lie down in are a version of Ireland or Scotland on a warm, sunny day. There are no people; it is just me and God and the expansiveness of the countryside.

Instead of being able to be fully present in reality, I can associate peace with taking a break from reality. When I think this way, peace is more of a rest stop along life's highway, not a fruit that can be experienced, even savored, all the time.

While peace certainly can be fostered in times of retreat, rest, and Sabbath, it is not only for those times. The original Hebrew sounds funny in a direct translation, so it is easy to miss that Psalm 23 isn't about rest stops but about life. As pastor Justin Alfred explains,

> The phrase, "He makes me lie down," comes from the Hebrew verb *yarbîsenî*, which is a Hiphil verb form in the imperfect tense. The actual root verb is *rābas*, which means "to stretch out and lie down." However, the Hiphil form of the verb indicates what is called "causative action"— that is, action that has been or is being caused to occur by someone—and the imperfect tense indicates action that is continuous and ongoing. Thus, a more literal translation of the first part of this verse would be, "He continually causes me to lie down in green pastures."[9]

Similarly, the verb *leads* in "he leads me" is in the Piel imperfect verb form. If your eyes are rolling, stay with me because this nugget is worth it. Bottom line is that the Piel imperfect verb form also emphasizes an ongoing, continuous action. So, God is continually leading you besides still waters. Though Psalm 23 never uses the word peace, this is what peace is: your soul continually lying down in green pastures and continually being led beside still waters regardless of the circumstances.

As I'm working on the chapter, the coronavirus known as Covid-19 is sweeping across the world. Hundreds of millions of children worldwide are using technology to continue with their classes. Millions of parents, teachers, and school officials are equally impacted by these children learning remotely. Because this happened around the lunar new year, daily I'm receiving texts from displaced teachers impacted and stressed by not "being home" and able to teach in person. Fuses are short. One of my friends who teaches in a country that has asked foreigners to leave if possible finds herself at a resort in another country spending hours in front of her computer recording lessons for her students. In a flurry of frustration, words were spoken to a coworker who happens also to be staying at the same resort. Words that can be apologized for, but the hurt still lingers and the closeness they felt for much of their shared exile is bruised. As my friend told me after apologizing to her coworker, "I hurt her comfort around me."

In a nutshell, that is one of the most accurate ways to express a lack of peace and a presence of fear, jealousy, distrust, and exhaustion: comfort has been hurt. Your thoughts or interactions are less peaceful.

Because Covid-19 impacted everyone, we all have our own stories of how our lives were disrupted. A common question that came out of the pandemic is, What does peace look like when it seems so much is out of our control?

INWARD SENSE OF COMPLETENESS

Which sounds better, freedom or partial freedom? If you're like most, the answer that popped up without even needing to give it much thought is *freedom*. I can picture Mel Gibson in *Braveheart* yelling, "Freedom!" One of the tricks of the enemy of your soul is to get you to settle for a limited sense of the freedom God has for you. Instead of outright twisting the truth, he obscures part of it.

Similar to joy, this fruit has been tied to outward circumstances. If I'm not on a crowded subway or if my teammate shows up to a meeting on time, I'm more likely to feel peaceful. And while it's true that I do not enjoy being on such a crowded subway that I can't escape an elbow pressed into my kidney, the truth is that if you live in a crowded city, you're going to have elbows in your space. You're probably more familiar with the Hebrew word *shalom* for peace than the Greek *eirene*. In the New Testament, *eirene* is used in the same sense as *shalom* in the Old Testament. Shalom embodies "completeness, fullness, or a type of wholeness that encourages you to give back—to generously re-pay something in some way."[10] The biblical sense of peace involves more of an inward sense of completeness or tranquility instead of an outward state between people or nations (or elbows).

Like a dry plant soaking up water, let the fullness of what shalom is seep into your soul. The more whole you are in mind and body, the more able you are to be present and involved in your life without being overcome by it. I don't mean to say that you won't have hard seasons, but even in the midst of crisis or helplessness, the sense that you are safe and that you will be completed by Christ *can* be true. It's out of the deep pool of walking with the Holy Spirit that you're enabled to respond generously and peacefully to a situation.

Yesterday as I worked on the above section, my writing time was anything but peaceful. Instead, it felt more like I was in a "peace laboratory" from God. I sensed God prompting me, *Can you really live this integrated "full fruit" life, experiencing all nine in the midst of reality? Writing about it is one thing; living it is another.*

A friend kept texting me. When she's in a bad place emotionally, she tends to spiral out of control and catastrophize about anything she can think of. She's also oriented to the past when it comes to time, and I am oriented to the future. In these spaces, she replays past conversations. She'd said a hurtful thing to another friend and kept berating herself. "Why am I so dumb?" "Why can't I learn?" "I have ruined everything." On and on it went. When she's in these bad places, sometimes I can love her well, and other times, well, other times, frustration wins out. Paul could have used me and these types of interactions as a contrast between walking in the flesh and walking with the Holy Spirit. Sometimes I'm willing to sacrifice my time in the name of love, I can experience joy (not that I'm happy for her, but I can see that our interaction *is* helping her and that gives me joy), and I'm able to interact out of the peaceful wholeness of my soul. But not yesterday.

Her focus on the past butted heads with my focus on the future. Since she had apologized to her other friend about her careless words, what else was there to do? While she replays and replays a situation or conversation, mining it for misery—if that's how I describe it, you can tell when I'm not in a great place either!—my patience wanes. We'll talk more about patience in the next chapter, but patience and peace feed each other. Because I was working on this book, I was aware of the future and that one day (today!) you would hold this book. My hope and prayer is that through these pages you'd grow in experiencing all of the fruit of the Spirit. But you could only read these pages if they get written! And with every flash on my phone screen that another text, or at times eight texts, had come in, my present kept interrupting my future.

My text responses may not have been unloving, but there was no joy in my responses to her and no peace in my heart. I didn't feel "shalom complete" as a person. Nor did I feel like I was continually lying down in green pastures or being led beside still waters. I felt that every dang text was a massive withdrawal from my peace reserves and a distraction from what I was trying to do. *How can I write about peace and the freedom this fruit gives when you will not leave me be?!* screamed every fiber of my being. After about two hours of this, I finally texted that I needed to work and would talk to her in a few days. Which I know triggers abandonment in her, but I texted it anyway as a signal that I was so beyond done. Sure enough, freak-out texts started lighting up my phone screen. Clearly, I was not exhibiting self-control or kindness (we'll get to those two in future chapters). Works of the flesh, about 5,000 points. Fruit of the Spirit? Maybe half a point?

WARNING LIGHTS

Later, on a walk, having gotten enough work done that I was depleted and needed to recharge, our interaction stayed with me. I was still stirred up inside even though my body was doing something that normally calms and replenishes me. I trusted God's timing and knew that He was trying to show me something about peace that I could only truly taste when I wasn't experiencing the peace that passes understanding. One of my mottos when it comes to negative feelings is to "feel your feelings, but don't feed them." In other words, often disappointment, betrayal, or hurt is a natural and appropriate response to a situation. For some of us, we actually may need to work on feeling those types of negative feelings. But we've all been in situations where we don't just *feel* hurt; we *feed* the hurt. Instead of processing the disappointment, we grow the disappointment. We nurture these feelings like Gollum in *The Hobbit* with his ring, which he called "my precious." If we feed the negative feelings long enough, they end up controlling us and, like Gollum, we turn into a shell of who it is that God made us to be.

What if the opposite should also be a motto when it comes to the fruit of the Spirit? "Feel the fruit, and then feed it." *How can I feed peace?* I wondered. In this case with my friend, I do love her. I want to experience peace within myself when we interact. I also want peace—a sense of wholeness in our friendship—between us. What God and I talked about as I walked through the snowy woods is that peace that depends on my interactions with others is built on a foundation that cannot hold what I'm asking it to hold. Yes, we all can, and should, invest in relationship skills. Let's learn about love languages, boundaries, healthy conflict resolution skills, and effective communication techniques. Growth in these areas will reap fruit too. But what if your mom is horrible with boundaries, or your dad has dementia, or your teammate's love language exhausts you? If you just try to muster up the will to "have more peace," this sounds like you are back to a shiny version of living by the flesh—trying to do something that comes out of *you*, not out of the Spirit.

A life of freedom isn't solely about doing something better, harder, or longer; yes, we are asked at times to sacrifice or to do something out of duty. But not always. Walking with the Spirit involves *discerning* more than *knowing*. Sometimes you'll be asked to endure longer with a friend, a team, or a situation than you want to. But sometimes a lack of fruit is a warning light on the dashboard of your life. A warning light that God uses to let you know that something needs to change.

In my case, when I place too much hope or expectation on my friend, I've handed my potential peace to her. It's tempting to externalize peace and place hope in the visa working out, the hospital having the right medicine, your teammate changing, you getting married or having a child. Even something as simple as the hoping the electricity stays on during a long-anticipated video chat with your family can externalize your source of peace. Feel the feeling, but don't feed it. Feeding the frustration keeps it external and doesn't allow for the peace that only comes from God to be as fully present as it could be. The lack of peace I experienced in myself as each text from my friend came in was more about me than about my friend.

God is growing in me the ability to recognize that lack of peace is an invitation to see where I may be out of step with Him or with what He has for me in a situation. Sometimes your lack of inner, God-given peace might indicate that you need to speak up in a situation. Sometimes it might mean that you need to hold your tongue. While I believe in and try to practice various spiritual practices such as silence, stillness, and solitude, I need to be wary of the myth that if I do these practices "right," I will fill up my fruit tank and have an abundance of love, joy, and peace for the day. This is another half-truth that tempts me to walk in my own flesh and to prove to myself and others how great I am.

Instead of viewing those practices as a stop at a gas station to fill up my tank, they are intended to build muscles so that in the midst of a trying situation I am more likely to turn to God than simply rely on my reserves.

WHAT ABOUT PEACE UNDER DISTRESS?

One of TIC's vice presidents was in town for new personnel orientation and planned to sit in on a session I was leading. Before the session started, he came to the front of the room and asked me how I was going to handle a particular piece of information from the home office. Tension had existed for a couple years between us, and I felt his approach was too aggressive and knew I was on the verge of saying something I would regret, so I turned and walked over to a colleague. I had about two minutes before the session started, and I was to present, of all things, a devotional. Most in the room probably hadn't noticed the interaction between us as they settled in their seats. And I'm sure no one but me noticed that he stayed only long enough to see if I handled the information in the way he thought it should be handled.

I hate the feeling of dissonance when I don't have the space to process something and need to put it in a box for the time being and move along. This was one of those times. As much as I was able, I put my stirred-up feelings in a box, turned to the room of excited folks new to the field, and shared the devotion. Later in the day, as I had space to process the interaction, the Holy Spirit convicted me that turning and walking away from a vice president wasn't appropriate and I needed to apologize. To this day, I don't know how I could have handled the situation differently. Even though I stand by my turning around so as not to escalate the situation, this is not normally how I behave. I knew I could at least acknowledge that walking away from a VP wasn't how he should be treated. It was an offering of peace that I could in good conscious give to him.

That evening all of the staff had dinner together at a restaurant. Near the end of the meal I went over to him and asked if we could step outside the room and talk. My intention was to use the principles of Matthew 18 and go to him alone without adding further fuel to our strained relationship. Because the group was having dinner in a private room, we stepped outside the door, and as I started to apologize, it was like the lid exploded off a pressure cooker, and what I thought was going to be a private apology suddenly became something very different. Over the next few minutes every grievance from the past few years was thrown at me, many that hadn't been spoken until that point. In the midst of our interaction I realized that this was a horrible "he said, she said" situation because we were alone. When I didn't back down on a question, he jumped to another and kept looking for an area that I would admit to one of the wrongs he'd been keeping against me?[11] Who would believe me that he rapid-fire attacked me?

After a few more minutes we ended our conversation, and I left the restaurant in shock and texted a colleague at the dinner that I wasn't coming back into the room. She came out and joined me in the cab and could tell that whatever had happened with the VP, it was bad. We both knew I was in a race against the VP to get to my boss first and that very likely my job was on the line. How did this happen? How could so much be lost in such a short period of time? Sure enough, I received an email from the VP as the cab moved through Beijing traffic. He uninvited me to represent TIC at an upcoming mobilization conference in America. At least I'd read the situation correctly and whatever he had direct control over with me, he was "firing" me from.

I kept calling my boss, but he didn't pick up. I also texted asking him to call me. I was shaking with adrenaline pulsing through my body as the cab arrived at our destination. Finally, I was able to connect with my boss. He already knew of the incident, and I'll never forget his sigh. I could picture his shoulders hunched over in sadness knowing what a mess the whole situation was. The only good news to come out of our conversation was finding out that Jesus had protected me and it was not, as I had thought, solely a "he said, she said" matter. The only person my boss trusted without hesitation had passed us on her way to the bathroom and saw our interaction. My boss's wife reported to her husband, my boss, how scary the interaction between the VP and I had been.

Because by now it was late in the evening, my boss and I set up a time to meet the next morning. As we discussed the situation the next morning, my boss wanted to get the VP and me together that day so that we would not "let the sun go down on our anger." Or at least not let another sun go down. I understood his sentiment. I also deeply loved and respected my boss and understood he was caught between the VP and me. For his sake, I said that I would meet with the VP, but the peace would be a fake peace at that point. We were too close to what had happened, and I didn't want to be physically near the VP yet, if ever. In his wisdom, my boss didn't push for us to meet that day. A few days later the VP got on a plane and headed to his next destination. Several months later, when he was back in town, we were able to meet with a mediator and process the incident.

Jesus is not after fake peace. Sometimes what is needed is space, wise counsel, and personal processing. I'm not talking about cases of abuse or other significant boundary violations; those need to be handled with professional input and awareness of laws and law enforcement. Of course, this can be even more complicated on the field with at least two countries' laws—those of passport country and host culture—to factor in. Because of these complexities, turning a blind eye to true abuse seems easier in the short run. To our shame, however, too many examples of abuse have occurred in cross-cultural work unchallenged or unaddressed.

In a different incident, I coached one of our member care personnel on an emergency trip to visit a team to address an incident between two women I'll call Tina and Stacy. Tina as not the easiest person to team with, nor at that point was she the most emotionally healthy. Stacy was livid with Tina and went to her apartment to confront her about an issue. When Tina opened the door, Stacy cornered her and violently shoved her. I'll be honest, for the teammates and the member care person, it was easier to sympathize with Stacy! Truth be told, they'd all probably wanted to shove Tina at one point or another. But what Stacy had done technically would have gotten her into the legal system in America if the officials had been involved. Stacy probably would have been court ordered to take anger management classes. But on the field, it was tempting for the team to downplay Stacy's actions instead of seeing Tina as the victim. I say again, Jesus isn't after fake peace. So, what does peace look like internally and between people in these types of complex situations?

As I've studied and thought about the fruit of the Spirit, I've noticed a tendency to think of all of them first through a lens of how they help with my interactions with others. *How can I be loving to others? What does joy look like in this situation with my landlord? What is my role in helping to restore peace?* None of those questions are bad or wrong, but notice within yourself where your thoughts and focus gravitate first when it comes to love, joy, and peace. God in His wisdom gives nine fruit so that there is space for upward, outward, and inward focus. With this expanded understanding, peace starts with you being complete and whole in your thinking, your emotions, and your focus on God; then it creates space for the shalom of God to flow through you to choices you make about when to address something and when to let it go, even what words and tone to use.

Peace is possible in the mundane and in the more extreme situations because nothing is outside of God. Over the week I have worked on this chapter, Covid-19 has morphed beyond anything I could have predicted a week ago. Where I live, most of society is shut down. What does peace—or any of the fruit—look like in a crisis? I come back to this truth: "What I am leaving with you is shalom—I am giving you my shalom. I don't give the way the world gives. Don't let yourselves be upset or frightened" (John 14:27 CJB). Jesus promises that peace is possible because He doesn't give peace as the world gives peace. The wholeness He brings starts before these situations so that in the midst of them we can experience it.

PAUL LOVES PREPOSITIONS TOO

A friend and I had a couple of days to kill after our annual conference in Thailand and decided to spend it reading by the hotel pool. I tend to be one of those readers who has several books going at once and jumps around in my reading. Now, don't think me overly spiritual, but I pulled out my Bible to get a bit of a head start reviewing Revelation since my small group was going to study it soon. Seeing as Revelation is near one of my favorite books, I got distracted and read Philemon first.

"Grace to you and peace from God" (Philemon 1:3). No surprise to find a variation of Paul's familiar greeting. So familiar I missed it. Until I read a variation in Revelation. That night at dinner I struck up a stimulating dinner conversation centered on the phrase "grace to you and peace from God." I was particularly interested in the prepositions *to* and *from*, emphasizing them like that as I spoke. I even pulled out my Bible and started flipping to different books, wondering aloud about the variations on the greeting. Is it any surprise Jane switched the subject to zombies? Problem is, I had as much interest in zombies as she did in Pauline greetings. We ended up having the most bizarre yet satisfying conversation in which I talked about prepositions, greetings, and their frequency in Scripture and Jane talked about zombies.

I don't come from a tradition that "passes the peace," and though I'd read and studied many of Paul's letters, I tended to skip over the introduction to get to the meatier stuff, viewing them more as a perfunctory version of "Dear Grandma and Grandpa, How are you? I'm fine."

Appearing eighteen times in the New Testament in one form or another, it's easy to tune out the greetings on the way to the good stuff. Turns out, these greeting *are* the good stuff. The most common rendition is "Grace and peace to you from God our Father and the Lord Jesus Christ." The simplest is in 1 Thessalonians 1: "Grace and peace to you." To Timothy, Paul includes "mercy," and Peter in his two letters adds "abundance," reminding me that they, too, lived real lives with annoying people, financial pressures, and their own failings.

Paul, in his "I will not play one side against the other and we have got to figure this out—like now!" approach, incorporates both Greek/Gentile *and* Hebrew culture. Grace from Greek and peace from Hebrew. He refused to use a separate greeting for each group and figured out a way to put his twist on a familiar social norm. He took a mundane, easy-to-overlook part of culture and expanded it to unite people and subtly point out that both groups, all people really, need grace and peace. "Grace to you and peace from God." The peace that passes all understanding isn't a zombie-like attribute that enables us to deal with those we encounter, be it teammates, family members, foes, or strangers. Ours is a God not of escape but of engagement.

After that dinner conversation, I researched and mulled over "grace and peace." The order is significant. Grace and then peace. Grace is given by God so that as we interact with one another, it's not based on our own merit or goodness. (Whew! Because if you're anything like me, we'd be playing Russian roulette with what might come out of me when left to my own devices.) But if we leave it at grace, it's easy to slip into the focus being on ourselves and experiences; adding "peace" brings the relational aspect into the mix as well. Even the letter to the Galatians has the "grace and peace" greeting. Paul knew he was going to write to them about the freedom they were forsaking when they returned to living by the flesh. He knew that God had so much more for them—and us—and that a life filled with the fruit of the Spirit results in freedom. Even here in the greeting, he starts to lay the seeds of freedom that is experienced in the combination of grace and peace. While it might have been a common way for Paul to start his letters, let's not become numb to how amazing God's heart is for you and me is.

As we come to the end of this section, let's pause here for a moment to remember that freedom begins with these habits of the mind that point upward. So far we've oriented ourselves upward, seeking to walk with love, joy, and peace. In the next section we turn our gaze outward as we explore how the fruit of the Spirit can be experienced in our interactions with others.

LET US PRAY

Grant me, O Lord, for your sake, through the work of your Holy Spirit, love for those I've come to serve and those I serve with, joy in the midst of the mundane and the miraculous of my life, and peace that starts within me and flows to others. Amen.

OUTWARD

PATIENCE

KINDNESS

GOODNESS

PATIENCE

A hot-tempered person stirs up conflict,
but the one who is patient calms a quarrel.
—Proverbs 15:18

Several years after I moved to China, my dad bought a used truck from a coworker and took up four-wheel driving as a hobby. My grandpa had an old red truck I loved to ride in when he took a load out to the dump. In my mind trucks were Grandpa, cars were Dad. Watching a hobby develop at a distance—more like listening to it over the phone—was odd. Quite quickly, it developed from "I bought Brad's truck" to "Your mother and I are four-wheeling on the weekends."

Dad bought a book about four-wheel trips in Colorado, and on the weekends he and my mom explored a new trail or path—I'm clearly not up on the lingo. (The whole four-wheeling thing seemed a bigger cultural leap to me than much of my life in China. *My parents are doing what?!*) So, it was no surprise when I was home that Dad asked if I wanted to go four-wheeling with them. They nicknamed the truck Lurch, which says all that you might need to know about our day.

Lurch was large enough for the three of us to fit in the front seat with me in the middle. To give you a picture of just how big

Lurch was, at one point on a bumpy trail, Dad put the truck in park, and he and I got out to build up the road with enough rocks for us to continue. Mom sat in the cab working on a crossword puzzle, absolving her of any possible responsibility for death from the absurdity. Jeeps we saw on the same road did not have to do manual road work and fit nicely on the trail.

Around noon we stopped for lunch, which was no small feat because of the hassle of hauling ourselves back into the tall cab and buckling in. Anyone else played the game "I'll lift my hip while you take your time getting your seat belt buckled?" Why do those five seconds feel like five hours? Buckled up and ready to go for the afternoon, my dad worked to get Lurch in gear. Next to me, Mom was fussing and muttering under her breath. When I asked her what was wrong, she said, "Your dad isn't driving the truck the way I would."

And just like that, I understood about 80% of the problems I have with other people. They don't drive the truck the way I would.

BEAUTIFULLY AND MADDENINGLY POSSIBLE

My dad wasn't doing anything dangerous or illegal, both legitimate reasons to want (and need) him to drive the truck differently. He was simply driving in a way that differed from how my mom would drive. Paul knew that interacting with others is one of the ways we are made in the image of God. It's also one of the areas we experience our brokenness most profoundly. Even as Jesus withdrew to spend time alone with His Father, the majority of His time was spent with others. Even though trucks didn't exist in the first century, I like to think that Paul had the three of us in mind when he shifts from fruit that can only come from God—love, joy, and peace—to fruit that we mainly need when interacting with each other.

Because this is a familiar passage, you know that patience, kindness, and goodness are the next three fruit grouped together. They focus on interacting with others, and since two of the three seem to highlight more obviously our "wonderfulness," I can sometimes fool myself into thinking that I'm ready to run with the Spirit, enough of this walking. Just think if Paul had started these three with kindness. Ah, yes, when I'm filled with love, joy, and peace, kindness being next might tempt me into thinking I am a lovely person. Or he could have launched this trio with goodness. But no, Paul doesn't start with either of these lovelier fruit. Instead, he joins us in Lurch's cab and says, "Friend, patience. You'll know the Holy Spirit is alive in you when you experience patience in this bumpy ride called life."

The Galatians had gone a bit off course and had forgotten that Christ came to offer freedom, not more rules. Yes, Christ came to unlock the shackles of rules and "shoulds," but look how comfortable the shackles feel. *A good cross-cultural worker should have better language skills than you do. A good cross-cultural worker should trust God more. A good cross-cultural worker should have more time for his teammate.* While you might need stronger language skills, more trust, or more time for a teammate, God never motivates only out of "shoulds." Freedom allows you to dig deeper and hold a bigger story. Freedom cultivates patience because of how patience sets you free, not because of what you should or shouldn't do. What can be confusing is that often "shoulds"—the best things we do for the sake of others—and freedom get tangled together. *Should* you make time for a teammate? I don't know, but I trust that the Holy Spirit is alive in you and will prompt you with how love, joy, peace, and patience work in the relationship with your teammate.

While looking at the first three fruit, we kept freedom in the forefront of our minds. Paul reminds all of his readers, those of his own time and those throughout history, including you and me, that Christ died in part for us to live a life of freedom. We once were slaves to sin, but now we are free. Though moving from a slave state is an event, it's also a process. Freedom means that we are free to love, experience joy, and have the fullness of peace. Freedom is our bass note added to the picture. It will continue to play throughout Paul's message and this book.

Earlier we touched on the fact that Paul intentionally used the phrase "the *fruit* of the spirit" instead of "*fruits* of the spirit." Like a cluster of grapes, these fruit are individual grapes that grow in a group. As I type, the autocorrection program on my computer keeps suggesting I choose either the phrases "these fruits" or "this fruit." English does not have a clear way to speak of different fruits within one plant other than a cluster. While spell check wants me to reconcile the tension by clarifying if I am talking about "this fruit" or "these fruits," God says, "Yes, both/and," beautifully demonstrating that we are capable of bearing all the fruit. Also maddeningly demonstrating that none of us get a free pass to skip, or ignore, the fruit (or fruits) that are hard for an individual.

WHAT OTHERS HEARD

Reading about grapes in the Scriptures, there is much that I, as a nonagrarian-culture person, could miss. We discussed earlier that by choosing to compare the indwelling of the Holy Spirit to grapes, God reminds us that we are capable of far more than we realize. We don't have to choose or settle for some of the fruit; all nine can coexist at the same time in the same person (my mind is still blown by this fact!). But this is not the only gem hidden in plain sight. Paul also chose grapes because the original recipients of the letter would have heard something you probably missed. I missed it too. When I taught a culture class to Chinese scholars visiting America, one of my favorite lessons to teach was baseball. More than any other sport, baseball has influenced the thinking and sayings of English. When a parent says to her daughter, "That's strike two," both know what she means even if neither has ever held a bat. So it is with grapes and Paul's original readers.

The Galatians understood that grapes produce fruit in rocky soil. A grapevine can grow in many environments, but in a more "favorable" environment without rocks, stones, and other impediments, they don't produce fruit. Instead, a vine happily grows lush green leaves. Okay, I don't know if a plant can feel happy, but that's the sense I get when I picture a vine growing up a trellis. Almost daily you can see the plant spread. If Paul compares us to plants, Jamie Goode, British author with a PhD in plant biology, makes the opposite comparison—plants to people:

> Making the vines struggle generally results in better quality grapes. It's a bit like people. Place someone in a near-perfect environment, giving them every comfort and all that they could ever want to satisfy their physical needs, and it could have rather disastrous consequences for their personality and physique. If you take a grapevine and make its physical requirements for water and nutrients easily accessible, then (somewhat counterintuitively) it will give you poor grapes.[12]

Like the recipients of the letter to the Galatians, we need to be reminded that the life of the Holy Spirit leads to freedom. By placing freedom in rocky soil, God gently places His hands on our cheeks and turns us from gazing at a fantasy to seeing our own faces squarely in the mirror. Left on my own, I am tempted to romanticize the conditions that will produce the sweet juicy fruit in me, believing that the idealized conditions will lead to idealized versions of myself. Early-morning Amy with her cup of tea and quiet preparation for the day is far more patient than later-in-the-day Amy when her plans are thwarted by the internet going out or a prolonged red light or a person who cannot pick up on social cues. It's tempting for me to believe that if only people and problems didn't come my way, I would be my true self.

As we consider patience, kindness, and goodness, we will focus on what those who heard this first already knew: we need the stones of life to produce fruit.

THE SPACE AN INCH PROVIDES

Going to the post office in Chengdu to mail a letter was the polar opposite of a joyful picking up of a package at the post office. Mailing a letter and picking up a package occurred in two separate buildings not even on the same block. The experiences were so different, it's hard to believe that the name "post office" applies to both experiences. When I received a package slip in the mail, joy and anticipation washed over me and I thanked our kind and merciful Lord. I wondered who the package was from and what goodies I would find inside. My biggest concern was if I would be able to attach the package with a bungee cord to the back of my bike.

But mailing a letter? The post offices in China are not only for mailing packages and letters; they are also for paying bills. So, picture the phone company, the utilities company, and the post office had a baby. Oh, and if you mailed a package, you had to show all of your contents before mailing. A person trying to mail a package had to unload the contents as the postal employees rifled through the carefully packed box to guarantee that contraband wasn't being mailed. One more detail to help you picture the chaotic scene: every stamp needed to be glued on individually. Next to each window was a glue pot, often dripping with glue and pieces of wood used to spread the glue. With all of this in mind, picture me just a few months into my time in Chengdu when my language skills were low, so low. The only affordable way to communicate with friends and family in America was through letters. I was in the middle of this swirling mass of humanity, holding a stack of letters in my hand and being jostled and shoved and pressed on from all sides. Because fresh air is good, the doors and windows were always open, but the freezing air was not helping my ability to cope.

I snapped.

In one of my less proud moments, I took my fleece mittens and started batting those around me.

Oh friend, I did. Even now I cringe when I recall swatting at the people behind me, to my right and to my left. *Get out of my space. Do not push me. Stop shoving.* My message was loud and clear with each desperate swing of a mitten. Thankfully, my inappropriate behavior did not cause a scene or an escalation, but in that moment, when the fruit of patience could not come from me, it came to me.

Paul had several options for a word that could be translated as "patience." When he chose *makrothumia*, he used a word that is not generally applied to having patience with things or events; instead, it is a word that refers to patience in regard to people.[13] It's the same word that is used in the New Testament to describe

God's and Jesus' attitude toward humanity (Romans 2:4; 9:22; 1 Timothy 1:16 1 Peter 3:20). God has the patience to bear with us and not cast us off. That afternoon in the post office, when I reached the end of myself and those around me were also almost too squished to take a step back, they offered me the few inches they could. Sometimes as we walk with the Spirit, in His mercy to us, the fruit that in that moment can't come *through* us comes *to* us.

SITTING ON THE GROUND

One of the urban myths that circulates among international travelers I chose to believe is that female border control workers are faster than male border control workers. From the moment I heard this customs tidbit, I acted as if it came from God's mouth to my efficiency-loving heart. Even in my jet-lagged stupor, when I hustle off a plane, I start to jockey my way as close to the front of the line as I can, scanning for a line with a female behind the glass. To say I am obsessed with efficiency is absurd because is there any other way to do something than efficiently?

But life with people is more often marked by waiting than by efficiency.

Job was a righteous man who had good friends. It's a familiar story that when they heard about his troubles, they met together first and then went as a group to see Job. His friends visited because they cared for Job and planned to sympathize with and comfort him. "When they saw him from a distance, they could hardly recognize him; they began to weep aloud, and they tore their robes and sprinkled dust on their heads" (Job 2:12). Love motivated them to show up and sit on the ground with Job for seven days and nights, not saying a word. It was Job who broke the silence, not his friends. Patience also encapsulates the steadfastness and staying power we see in these three friends.

Patience personified is a group of friends who show up and sit with you for seven days. I imagine that Eliphaz the Temanite, Bildad the Shuhite, and Zophar the Naamathite didn't mind sitting on the floor in silence. Sometimes, though the stones in the soil of life are real, the fruit comes easy. Often, when a friend is suffering, there's no place you'd rather be than by their side.

Sometimes the patience a situation calls for is this kind of patience. And though it may not be easy and it may cost you, it isn't hard to muster up steadfastness and the staying power a moment calls for. I was on the phone with my sister reviewing the details of her upcoming trip to visit me in Beijing with two of her young daughters. The conversation and my excitement were interrupted by an early-morning knock at the door. Asking my sister to wait a minute, I answered the door. Jenn was in her final month of pregnancy and was staying in TIC's guesthouse. Her husband, Paul, was scheduled to return to Beijing the following week in plenty of time for the baby's birth. "Amy, I heard you used to be a labor and delivery coach. I've been timing my contractions the last few hours, and I think I'm in labor. Paul is trying to get a ticket to Beijing. Would you go to the hospital with me?"

I told my sister goodbye and invited Jenn in. As we talked, it became even more apparent that she was in labor and that even though it was a rare snow day in Beijing (translation: traffic was beyond awful), we'd be headed to the hospital. I called the prearranged driver to pick us up within the hour. About thirty minutes before we arrived, I thought to call the hospital and give them a heads-up that we were coming in. Around nine o'clock we pulled up to the front door of the hospital. Our colleague Laura, who had come to help out with random tasks, paid the driver while

Jenn and I walked into the hospital and straight up the staircase to the labor and delivery ward.

We were ushered into a room, and Jenn was handed a hospital gown. What comes next might sound impossible. If I hadn't seen it with my own eyes, I might think I was exaggerating for dramatic flair, but this is what happened. The nurse checked to see how far along Jenn was and barely had time to call the doctor. Baby Timothy shot out between her legs onto the bed. It was 9:15 a.m. Shock mingled with joy. By 9:30 a.m. the nurses and doctor had cleaned up, verified that Baby Timothy was healthy, and exited stage left. Thirty minutes after we'd pulled up to the hospital, the birth was over and the three of us were left alone with this precious newborn.

Her husband, Paul's, flight hadn't taken off yet, so as he boarded the plane, he found out that instead of hurrying for the birth of his son, he was hurrying to *meet* his son.

Stunned, we rotated between shock and awe. Was it really mere moments before that we three we were in a van with pauses in our conversations every time Jenn had another strong contraction? Beijingers are not great drivers in the snow, and even though the trip took longer than normal, the snow created the sense we were traveling in a poem. We kept shaking our heads; Timothy could have been born in that van. Now that all the excitement was over, there was nothing to do but sit and talk. So we did. At first we were compelled to retell the birth story to each other . . . slowly working out what we all knew but still could not quite believe in the retelling.

We talked and talked and took turns holding Timothy. As we waited for a text that Paul's plane had landed and then for reports about where he was in traffic, Jenn shared the story of their firstborn, Joshua, who was back at the guesthouse with a babysitter. Suffice it to say, God in His mercy took every detail from her first birth experience and reversed it. Most of that morning we were left alone. Any other time I would find the lack of checking on us by the nurses negligent, but after the traumatizing treatment by nurses at the first birth, the absence seemed divinely arranged by God.

In the early afternoon, Paul arrived, and as he held Timothy, we retold the story again and again. The drive. The birth. The different experience from Jenn's first birth. Every detail from every angle. I thought they might want Laura and me to leave so they could be alone, but when we said we would go, they asked us to stay. Sometimes joy and shock need to be shared. So we stayed.

On the long and slow cab ride home, Laura needed to debrief the day. She was young and it was her first birth. So we talked.

When I returned home, what was my night was now my sister's morning, and I sent her a short email about my day. Sometimes you sit on the ground with a friend, like Job's friends did. And sometimes you sit in traffic or a hospital room. I hadn't planned to spend the entire day ignoring the work that needed to be done before my family arrived. The freedom that comes with patience is the ability to open our hands and say, "Not my will but yours, God." Hopefully seeing any interruption as more of a redirection.

PATIENCE WITH GOD

Wouldn't life be lovely if all situations that require patience involved getting to hold a newborn, gazing in awe while demands of the day go unanswered. But more often, this fruit is truly born out of the rocks that trip you up, get in your way, or, like a pebble in your shoe, cause you to wince when you step on it. What do we do with the situations that require patience for more than just a day or short season, when with the psalmist you cry, "How long, LORD? Will you forget me forever?" (Psalm 13:1)?

Like you, I have situations and people I've prayed for years for God to change. For God to intervene. For God to do something, anything! And yet it seems like He is silent or, worse, doesn't care as much as I do. Which I know in my head is not true, but my heart still wonders.

At the core of patience is waiting. And I hate to wait. Too often I associate waiting with inefficiencies (see above customs tip). When I moved to China, it both scared and thrilled me that many traffic signals were approached as suggestions, not firm rules. Finally, a place where my love of making forward progress was a chaotic reality. As I write these words, the world seems to be in a collective holding pattern. How will we know when the coronavirus is "done"? Will the racial injustices experienced around the world that have sparked waves of demonstrations lead to lasting change? Though you may read this with the pandemic in the rearview mirror, you have your own situations that leave you wondering when they will be over. Or wondering why we're having the same conversations again and again. "How long must I wrestle with my thoughts and day after day have sorrow in my heart?" (Psalm 13:2).

"If in English we had an adjective 'long-tempered' as a counterpart to 'short-tempered,' then *makrothymia* could be called the quality of being 'long-tempered.'"[14] Romans 8 has a verse that is both true and commonly misused. You've probably heard it so many times you go on autopilot when it starts. "And we know that in all things God works for the good of those who love him, who have been called according to his purpose" (Romans 8:28). Because it's been plucked out of context and used as a platitude so often, I find myself recoiling a bit when I hear it. On its own, it is too simple to hold up to the big questions I have. But back up a few verses and read:

> We know that the whole creation has been groaning as in the pains of childbirth right up to the present time. Not only so, but we ourselves, who have the firstfruits of the Spirit, groan inwardly as we wait eagerly for our adoption to sonship, the redemption of our bodies. For in this hope we were saved. But hope that is seen is no hope at all. Who hopes for what they already have? But if we hope for what we do not yet have, we wait for it patiently. (Romans 8:22–25)

Groaning. This captures how I feel when I think about all the prayers and hopes for the world that have not been answered. The world is wonderful and glorious and full of redemption. But it's also unfair and ugly and laced with brokenness. How do we live with both realities? We wait, as Paul said, patiently. And while this might sound like a circular line of logic leading nowhere, this is where God reminds us that He *is* at work for the good of those who love Him. This isn't a line from a Hallmark movie where the outcome's a foregone conclusion; instead, this is a promise to you and to me in the midst of our groans. I need to remind myself that God is at work for the good . . . not the easy, not necessarily the quick solutions, but He is at work and it's good. Patience can be the sweet fruit where we, made in His image, become more long-tempered.

WEEDS, NEIGHBORS, AND ME

The house I live in shares fences with five neighbors. Good news is that four out of the five maintain their yards similarly to us.

They water and mow the grass and enjoy being outside. Four out of five are good odds. But the fifth neighbor? He ignores his gardens and yard. On the one hand, it's his yard and his choice. On the other hand, the thistle patch that has overtaken his garden doesn't understand the word *fence*.

Most weekends, I dig up between forty and sixty young thistles in our yard. I know how many because I'm so annoyed, I count. Frustration has even led me to lean over the fence in a futile attempt to root out the large thistles. Surely, if I kill enough of the parents, maybe the breeding problem will be solved, right? On the rare occasion when the neighbor isn't home, I've even jumped the fence and weeded.

Nothing I do has reduced the number of thistles on my side of the fence. Instead, God is using the annoying thistles to transform me. As I pull, God reminds me that while it's important to have fences and personal boundaries, they are not the be-all and end-all. Your stuff is going to impact me, and my stuff is going to impact you. We can't be in relationship without our "stuff" showing up in other people's lives. This tangible weekly reminder is *Amy, deal with your stuff.*

God also uses the thistles to remind me to tend my own life faithfully because smaller stuff is easier to deal with than big stuff. On the weeks that I don't get around to weeding, annoyingly—oh how annoying the whole situations is!—the thistles don't care and they happily keep growing. Annoyingly, but not surprisingly, when I return to weed, their roots are deeper, their prickles larger, and there are more of them. Argh!

And finally, the thistles remind me that much of life with others isn't once and done. Life has solvable and unsolvable problems. Wisdom comes in knowing the difference. Until I have a new neighbor who values ridding his or her garden of thistles as much as I do, this is going to be an ongoing situation.

Enter patience.

If Paul lived next to my neighbor, these thistles could be the unnamed thorn in his flesh. Even though Paul asked God to remove the thorn, He didn't. No matter how well you "tend your own lawn," you'll always have neighbors and teammates and family members. You were made for relationships. When I think of my dear friends and family, I cannot imagine life without them. Yet even with them, daily I need patience . . . and they need it with me.

Patience isn't only for my relationship with God and others; it's for my relationship with myself too. In Romans 7 Paul asked the age-old question, *Why do I do the things I don't want to do and don't do the things I want?* Just like with the thorn, there are no easy answers, which is simultaneously annoying and honoring. Annoying because you and I are not robots, and it's okay to have emotional reactions to situations and people and culture. Honoring because it acknowledges the history, complexities, and messiness of our lives and locations. Although over the years the ways in which I need patience with myself has shifted, I've yet to have a stage of life when I haven't needed it.

Life in the Spirit is a life marked by freedom *and* lived in rocky soil. Though I groan as I pull thistles because life is at times repetitive, at times hard, it's also fresh and fulfilling. Patience equips us for a rich life with others that includes truck rides and shared fences. But patience isn't enough when it comes to working and living with others; kindness helps us to show up and interact with others in ways that we can be proud of. Our next chapter will explore this equally necessary fruit of the Spirit.

LET US PRAY

Grant me, O Lord, for your sake, through the work of your Holy Spirit, love for those I've come to serve and those I serve with, joy in the midst of the mundane and the miraculous of my life, and peace that starts within me and flows to others.

Add to these fruit that flow from You patience, that I may be long-tempered with those I interact with today. Amen.

KINDNESS

Whoever pursues righteousness and kindness will find life,
righteousness, and honor.
—Proverbs 21:21 ESV

I grew up in a rafting family. From a young age I learned how to paddle through rapids, work together with fellow rafters, and bail out a boat that had taken on water. We owned our own raft, but sometimes we'd go with a professional company and be led by a guide down a new river. When rafting with a guide, every so often the guide would lead the raft to an eddy on the side of the river. When you eddy out, it's a chance to briefly check how everyone's doing and to regroup.

Midway through this book, let's "eddy out" and briefly check how you're doing. As we redefine fruitfulness from being primarily a measure of your ministry that focuses on an external metric to an outflowing from within you, it's still tempting to internalize a checklist. You might find yourself thinking, "Okay, today I need to be loving, joyful, peaceful, patient, and kind." Check, check, check. Living up to the letter of the law and all the while missing the, pun intended, spirit of what God has for you. If you feel more like you are in a fruit-filled food fight with yourself, the good news of the gospel is for you today. God is kind.

In China most people didn't own a car, so when I shopped, I could only buy as much as I could carry. Returning from the market overloaded, I needed to stop every so often and set my bags down; if a friend saw me, they would offer to help. Not once did they see me and fail to offer to carry a bag or two if they were carrying less than I was. Why? Kindness. Now, the analogy can only go so far because we all carry loads that others may or may not see. Even if I am heavy laden with my own problems, I want close friends to share their burdens with me because I care about them.

At this point in the book, my hope is that you're feeling encouraged about God and the life He has for you. More hopeful about the truly full life He has for you, not just the in-theory life. I'm praying you're encouraged that God isn't asking you to rank your top and bottom fruit because He wants you to have all of them.

But I also hope you're relieved that God isn't clueless about how hard life can be. He isn't unaware of injustice or the stresses you face. He isn't asking you to suck it up, shake it off, or downplay where you've been hurt. Instead, the fruit we find smack-dab in the middle of the list and in the middle of our messy lives is kindness. God could have placed this fruit anywhere in the list, but He chose to put it in the middle of the three fruit that are outward focused. Kindness, both to and from others, is like a cool drink on a hot afternoon. It says, "I might not be able to do anything about your woes, but I see you and I'll do what I can not to add to them." Kindness reminds us that we're not animals or machines. We are humans, made in the image of God.

The Greek word used in Galatians is *chréstotés*—and it taps into the idea that God is good. When we behave toward others in a way that is good, we're acting on our true God-given nature. One of the ways chréstotés can be translated is "useful kindness" that "meets real needs, in God's way and in His timing."[15] *Useful kindness.* Take a moment to savor that phrase. We've all had times when someone is kind and then you get the sensation, "Wait a minute, you want something." And sure enough, your daughter wants your phone or a local friend wonders if you can lend them money. Whether it is something as simple as a phone or complex as a request for money, true kindness isn't about getting. Instead, it's kindness that is useful to the person. It lightens their load, let's them know they are not alone, or shows them they are thought of.

EXCEPTIONS AND ROCKS

I like the idea of being a kind person. I want to be someone who's kind to others. But the truth is that I want to be kind when it's convenient for me or when it doesn't cost me much. And while saying a kind word, or waiting to hold the door, or taking the time to wish a friend happy birthday is meaningful, that's just scratching the surface. Let's return to the conditions under which grapes are fruitful. A grapevine is a fairly forgiving plant because it can grow in both good and rocky soil. But as I touched on earlier, if the soil is good, the vine won't go to the effort of bearing fruit.

[Give the grapevine] a favourable environment and it will choose to take the vegetative route: that is, it will put its energies into making leaves and shoots. Effectively, it is saying, 'This is a fine spot, I'm going to make myself at home here'. It won't be too bothered about making grapes. But make things difficult for the vine, by restricting water supply, making nutrients scarce, pruning it hard and crowding it with close neighbours, and it will take the hump. It will sense that this is not the ideal place to be a grapevine. Instead of devoting itself to growing big and sprawling, it will focus its effort on reproducing itself sexually, which for a vine means making grapes.[16]

In other words, feeling comfortable and unchallenged, the grapevine will grow leaf after leaf but no fruit. The rocky soil forces the vine to grow deep roots, searching for water and nutrients, and creates conditions where the plant produces fruit. But the conditions can get too hard. Too much stress and the vine either takes longer to ripen or begins to wither. We humans are the same. Too much of a good thing can lead to laziness or a sense of entitlement; too little can foster generational cycles that are hard to break.

The more I learn about grapes, the more I appreciate Paul's use of the grape metaphor in his letter to the Galatians. If life is too smooth, sadly, like the grapevine, I won't go to the effort of *truly* abiding in Him. I know the "good Christian answers" that let me coast. But reality is that life never seems to be smooth with no stressors for long. You don't need me to tell you that life on the field is littered with rocks. I recently reread a stack of my old newsletters. In one of them I wrote the following,

This spring several of us in leadership had an a-ha moment when we realized we use the word "exception" . . . shall we say, a lot. Planning for new personnel to come to the field has been full of *exceptions* due to the H1N1 disease. This spring we had restricted travel due to the *exceptions* in the economy. Last year it was the Olympics that caused *exceptions*. Earlier SARS caused a lot of *exceptions*. Looking back, three of the last six years have been *exceptional*. Even those who are not strong in math can easily calculate that three out of six is 50 percent!

This realization forced us to sarcastically ask ourselves, When did the exception become the rule? Riffing on the classic line from the movie *The Princess Bride*, when have we cried "inconceivable," or in our case "exceptional," one too many times? Sheepishly we had to admit that 50 percent didn't seem to constitute an exception.

Since rereading this newsletter, I've been wondering if the words *normally, special,* and *should* are codes for "rocks."

Normally it takes a couple of hours for the electricity to come back on.

It *should* take six months to get a visa.

This is a *special* regulation until after the national government meets.

In each situation, you know there's little you can do except—an exception, get it?—wait. But in every case, a little bit of kindness goes a long way. The thoughtfulness of a neighbor who checks in to make sure you're okay. The visa officer who shares the little she knows and is willing to stay on the phone until you've asked all of your questions . . . even though she can't answer any of them. Your teammate who validates your frustration in this season. Your neighbor, the visa officer, and your teammate's kindness is *useful* to your soul. If patience gives you endurance to bear with one another over time, kindness makes your interactions less isolating.

THE BACKSTORY

You've probably heard of the phrase "practice random acts of kindness," but you might not know the history. It's in reaction to the phrase "random acts of violence and senseless acts of cruelty."

In an effort to combat the violence and cruelty she was witnessing in the world, writer Anne Herbert wrote "Practice random acts of kindness senseless acts of beauty" on a place mat in a Sausalito, California, restaurant in 1982.[17] It spread to bumper stickers and in 1993 Herbert's book *Random Acts of Kindness* was published, setting off a chain reaction. You've probably heard of "random acts of kindness" no matter where you are in the world because many newspapers wrote about it, hundreds of radio stations (remember, this was 1993) devoted airtime to the cause, and a college professor gave a class assignment to go out and practice a random act of kindness, which unleashed even more stories.[18]

It seems a modern-day David-versus-Goliath situation. Kindness and beauty go up against violence and cruelty. It might be naive to think something as simple as kindness can make a difference. Yet . . . there *is* something compelling about kindness. Can you imagine if she had written "Practice random acts of patience and senseless acts of self-control"? Chances are, no bumper stickers, books, or class assignments would have followed!

While I'm grateful that Anne Herbert saw a problem and acted, I have to admit that this phrase has formed me in ways that might put me "fruit of the Spirit" adjacent instead of clearly walking with the Spirit. I'm prone to drop the word *practice*. For a book title, I understand that *Random Acts of Kindness* is punchier, but if we're not careful, it can let us off the hook a bit. Normally "practice" and "random" are not ideas that go together. If something is random, there's no intentionality. I have yet to hear one of my nieces say, "I accidentally practiced the piano today." Sitting at the piano is an act of intentionality. When Katy switched from percussion to the trumpet, she was behind other trumpeters her age. Being in a musical family, the idea that she'd need to practice the trumpet was nothing new, and she did. But about a year into playing the trumpet, she kicked her practicing into another gear and spent hours in the basement. Much to Katy's and her band teacher's shock and delight, those hours alone paid off when she made it into the all-county band and the all-state band. Like an instrument, kindness is something we can practice and get better at.

Let's be honest, life on the field can be random. On a flight in China I was sitting in the window three or four rows back from the front of the cabin. When it came time for drinks, I had decided on a cup of tea, which seemed to be the drink of the flight. When the air hostess (as they're called in China) handed each passenger his or her drink, she warned each of us to be careful because it was hot. I asked for my tea and expected the same gentle admonition in Chinese. Instead, as she placed the cup in my hand, she smiled and in the clearest English said just one word:

Enjoy.

As I took it from her, I had the sensation that she was speaking for Another. With assurance, clarity, and direct eye contact, I was commanded to *enjoy*. In that random moment I sensed that I was to *enjoy* more than just the tea. Her "order" startled me for a moment because it was undeniably clear . . . and simple! One word is not easy to get lost in, that's for sure. I was aware that I'd received a clear command that I wasn't to take lightly. Sipping my tea, I tried to focus on the taste in my mouth, the warmth of the liquid, even on the book I'd been reading. *Enjoy.* While I can't say that from that moment on I "enjoyed" every moment of my business trip, I can say that the word *enjoy* became a refrain for a season and helped to focus my thoughts.

Since violence can seem random, it does the heart good to think acts for good can just as randomly happen. Because the original idea of *Random Acts of Kindness* was for a stranger to do something that brings another happiness, the idea of kindness can inadvertently be watered down. It's a one-time act with people you don't know for a momentary dose of happiness. Though my interaction on the plane led to a longer ripple effect than a typical interaction with an air hostess, I've been on countless other flights where I can't recall what was said to me when I was handed my drink. No doubt the majority of the interactions have been pleasant. But the enemy of connection loves to water down a gift from God and have us think that kindness is random and between strangers. But this fruit is evidence of the Spirit alive in you, and it can be cultivated. Think of it this way: acts of kindness are tendons and sinews holding a body together. They're powerful and they make a difference.

MORE THAN ONCE AND DONE

Kindness also helps unbearable situations be more bearable. Sometimes kindness is one-to-one. Sometimes what may be a simple act of God's kindness, shown by one person to you, joins a gentle steady rain of kindness. One of the greatest frustrations on the field is computer problems. Not being overly techie, I didn't know how to explain the computer problem I was having to TIC's IT person; I took a picture and captioned it "Friendly Fire." Between three to four times, and some days up to twenty times a day, my screen would become a series of vertical stripes that alternated between black, blue, red, and white. If I happened to be listening to music or a podcast when it froze, it sounded as if my computer was shooting a semiautomatic rifle at me. Rebooting temporarily solved the problem. My member care job involved six trips or more a semester visiting people in their homes. So computer problems were both maddening and freeing; there was no point in lugging a computer that was more like a paperweight around China.

Thankfully, when I traveled to Lhasa, Tibet, one of our IT people was in Beijing waiting for the birth of his first child. With nothing else to do, he planned to try to fix my computer while I was gone. Blissfully, I went off to Tibet, grateful for the help in my time of need.

A week later a happy Amy returned to Beijing, smiling at the memories I'd made of helping people sort through life, prepare for a home assignment, and make other plans for the future. Though the week was doable without a computer, I sure missed mine and was eager to be reunited with it. While I was gone, a little someone decided to make a surprise arrival and my computer was in the exact same state. Sadly, her worst day (referring to my computer and not the new baby!) was on Tuesday when I wanted to listen to the Monday night Broncos game. I restarted my computer what felt like five hundred times trying to listen to the game. It was an effort in futility, as I kept hoping just one more try would make a difference. It didn't.

Hope came later in the week in the form of the head of IT traveling to Beijing for his monthly IT trip on Friday and Saturday. I left for Hong Kong, my next trip, grateful for the help I was about to receive in my time of need. After a whirlwind few days I returned to Beijing, curious as to the state of my (sometimes) computer, (sometimes) paperweight.

My computer, with help from the head of IT, wrote me a note apologizing for the trouble she'd caused and assured me that according to the head of IT she was better than ever. Waves of relief and joy flooded over me as I turned on the computer and started to download email. Within five minutes the screen froze, and my joy froze in frustration too. I took it as a sign to go to bed and deal with the situation in the morning. If the sheep know His voice, my computer seems to know my touch. Though I didn't fully understand the problem, something was broken related to the video driver. I desperately wanted a working computer for my next trip—meetings at our headquarters in America. But I didn't have any options other than to trust my computer to coworkers in the Beijing office to work with the computer dealership while I was gone. So, for the third time in a row, I traveled on a work trip without my computer. (Silent scream.)

In maddening situations that seem to go on forever, the upside was that as I cried more tears than should be shed over a machine, many people were kind to me. Each prayer, email, caring text, lent computer, and knowing look might have been a small gesture for that person. But for me they worked together to form a support net that held me and reminded me that I wasn't suffering unnoticed.

LESSONS FROM A CAT

This chapter started with a verse from Proverbs: "Whoever pursues righteousness and kindness will find life, righteousness, and honor" (Proverbs 21:21 ESV). What caught my attention was the verb *pursues*. My childhood cat, Patches, had a saggy belly that led people to ask how many litters she had delivered . . . only to find out she was a he and the answer was zero. Patches was a sight to behold when he saw something moving in the grass. He crouched down and was laser focused, creeping forward with an intensity that said, "You are mine!" To me, Patches is what pursuit looks like. True pursuit is clear on the task at hand and oblivious to the commentary of those around—even the laughter of your family with your saggy belly. Sorry, Patches!

If the idea of *pursuing* drew me to the verse, what kept me chewing on it was the idea that anyone can pursue righteousness and kindness. On the field, that means whether it's your first month or your twenty-seventh year, you can pursue kindness; if you're knee-deep learning a new language, teaching your children, meeting with government officials (or all three), you can pursue kindness. Kindness is for you on the days when all is right with the world and days when, if you were offered a plane ticket out, you'd take it without hesitation. This is the paradox of growing as a Christian: it is the work of the Holy Spirit in you *and* your intentional participation. Kindness is both evidence of God at work in you *and* of your obedience in thought and action as a child of God.

Why do you pursue kindness? Is it just for the sake of the one you are kind to? Here's the beauty of this proverb: whoever (that's me and that's you) pursues kindness (like a stalking cat) will find . . . life. Maybe your kindness will not be noticed, or maybe it will be met with gruffness. The promise isn't that your kindness is a quarter in life's vending machine and if you press B13 you will get exactly what you expect. The promise is that in the mysterious workings of God, when you pursue kindness, you—not just the person you're being kind to—*will* find life. Sometimes the "life" that is offered is being proud of how you handled a situation, that you noticed a need and responded to it, or were willing to sacrifice for someone. Start looking for the life that you experience when you're kind; it's there, my friend.

Let me briefly say that pursuing kindness isn't to be confused with allowing an abusive person to be abusive in any format. It isn't about having no boundaries or too rigid of boundaries with dysfunctional people. Pursuing kindness is about following the prompting of the Holy Spirit. He might have you stay up late and listen to your teammate vent about a situation, or He might say that you need to go to bed so you can be well rested for the next day (and for the people you'll need to be kind to in the morning). Pursuing kindness isn't a formula; it is an opportunity for wisdom and discernment (which is both freeing and maddening!).

Below I have a series of questions that you can simply read through. If one of the questions jumps out at you, spend time journaling or praying about it. This week you could also use these questions with your family over dinner or at a team discussion.

— What does it look like to be a person who pursues kindness?
— How can I pursue kindness with my tone?
— How can I pursue kindness with my body language? How do I need to adjust my nonverbal communication in my host culture? How do I need to adjust it when I visit my passport culture?
— How can I pursue kindness by continuing to learn about my host language, history, and culture? What does this look like the first few years in a country? What does it look like when I've been here three to ten years? More than ten years?
— How can I pursue kindness with a child who is in a difficult phase?
— How can I pursue kindness with a teammate who is difficult to love?
— How can I pursue kindness with people I don't share a language with?
— How can I pursue kindness with my supporters? My organization?
— How can I pursue kindness with coworkers when we face a difficult situation?

— How can I pursue kindness when I'm in Country 2 and I would rather be in Country 1 on the field?
— How can I pursue kindness when I am too hot or too cold?
— How can I pursue kindness when I'm in traffic or on public transportation?
— How can I pursue kindness with myself?
— How can I pursue kindness with my spouse? With my family?
— How can I pursue kindness when I'm flourishing? When I'm floundering?

These questions aren't meant to heap guilt on you but to give you a chance to see how kindness can be woven into your actual life. Sometimes a situation is difficult and there are no easy answers. My mom once mailed me four cheap tiaras in a care package just for fun. Those tiaras would occasionally make an appearance at the office when one of my colleagues would call for a "tiara talk." Tiara talks were born when four of us had a tricky contract situation with a partner Chinese university. It was tempting to think that all was hopeless and we would never find a solution that the school would accept. On a whim, I suggested tiaras for the meeting (yes, I was *that* teammate, just a little bit crazy). It turns out that, while having a meeting where the stakes are real, looking at colleagues, both local and expat, wearing tiaras helps. It's hard to get bogged down in hopelessness when you are earnestly working and wearing what was meant to be a child's toy. Tiara talks were saved for only the most complex, dicey situations, and they might not work for you, but they were a tangible way we could pursue kindness toward our school partners, our teacher partners, and each other. How can you pursue kindness in your life?

We're following the order of the fruit that Paul used, so we started with our eyes on God when we looked at love, joy, and peace. In this section we're two-thirds of the way through the fruit that is directed outward. These three fruit equip us to work with others from different vantage points and, like the grapevine, bear fruit in rocky situations. Patience helps us hold our ground and remain willing to stay in the messy middle of a situation. Kindness connects us to others and keeps us from drifting into isolated silos. But this trio of fruit is incomplete without goodness, which we'll explore in the next chapter.

LET US PRAY

Grant me, O Lord, for your sake, through the work of your Holy Spirit, love for those I've come to serve and those I serve with, joy in the midst of the mundane and the miraculous of my life, and peace that starts within me and flows to others.

Add to these fruit that flow from You patience, that I may be long-tempered with those I interact with today, and kindness that is useful to them and life-giving to me. Amen.

GOODNESS

God saw all that he had made, and it was very good.
—Genesis 1:31

I love the repeated refrain that starts the creation story: It was good. It was good. It was good. It was good. It was very good. The stories we tell form us, in part because they create neural pathways in our brains. So, look afresh at our creation story in the Bible and how this story forms us as children of God. From the beginning goodness echoes. After separating the land from the water, God could have declared the land and the water vast or beautiful; instead, He chose *good*. When the waters teemed with life and birds flew, He could have marveled at the variety; instead He said they were *good*. When the land produced living creatures, God could have mentioned their speed, agility, or mass; instead, He said they were *good*. And ultimately, when God made humans in His likeness, He blessed us with this declaration: *very good*.

The story of our goodness forms us.

Or it should. But just open the morning news: natural disasters, economic collapse, failing schools, rampant injustice, abuses of power, and, if elections are being held, it's often "the most contentious race ever seen." Does that sound *good*? Even on our best days, the choices we make and decisions we face could be described as anything but good. Is this lettuce safe to eat? How do I get the government to sign the form if I'm not willing to pay a bribe? Are we harming our children by placing them in local schools? Are we doing more social development harm by homeschooling them? How can I help my newly believing friend navigate a culture that is hostile to Christian beliefs?

All of the questions swirling around you share a root question: how can you get back to the good part of the story? While there's no one simple way, there is a simple place to start: a posture of offense. Not being offensive, but instead of *reacting* to the terrible around us, we can *respond* to it. Goodness today feels more like it has switched from playing offense to playing defense. You can sense it in any stance that says, "I'm going to protect mine before you take it from me." Goodness is the fruit that moves this approach to a more open one. The goodness of Jesus opens its arms and walks toward complex problems, saying, "I'm not afraid that your darkness will overtake me. I'm going to trust that God is good, that I'm a part of that goodness, and that His light can shine here."

In the last chapter, we talked about "useful kindness." If kindness is how we *can be*, goodness is who we *are*. In Greek, kindness, goodness, and gentleness are often interchangeably translated, which shows how intertwined they are. Though goodness may be hard to define, like U.S. Justice Stewart famously said when ruling on whether or not something is obscene, "I know it when I see it."[19] So, even though it is hard to pin down, goodness—*agathōsýnē*—is related to kindness but differs in that goodness is more active. In particular, the idea of goodness compared to kindness in Greek is that goodness is often directed toward a person or situation that doesn't merit action. The primary idea seems to be "generosity that springs from kindness."[20] Or kindness is action.

From the beginning of time, we knew goodness. We were declared good. I believe in goodness, and at times I am tempted to think that true goodness was in Eden and will be in heaven, but here? In this messy world? Not likely.

But what if I'm wrong?

What if goodness is deep in our cells and souls? What if it can be in our interactions too? What if it can be in our interactions each other, the conversations we have, and the ways we show up in the world? Now, that's a world I want to be a part of, and I bet you do too.

BEYOND THE SURFACE

What parent or babysitter hasn't hissed, "Be good," loud enough for a child to hear yet under their breath without drawing attention from onlookers? To this day, if I close my eyes, I can hear my mother snap her fingers and give us the eye when she was on the phone and one of us girls was being a bit too loud. That snap was a warning that we needed to change course immediately. And we did. Learning that you can control yourself and how to control yourself is part of growing up. But for some Christians, the idea of being good is an inch deep and a mile wide. Too often, changing our outside behavior has been emphasized over changing our inside motivations, desires, or needs. True goodness moves beyond describing people as good based on what they *do* to describing them based on who they *are*.

Maybe this is akin to psychobabble or a game of semantics. You know the bad you've done. You know the ways you have disappointed and hurt friends and family. You know when the good you meant to do wasn't the way you ended up responding. Being good isn't something where you simply need to try harder or think better or give yourself a motivational talk about. No matter how hard you try, life is still hard. Suffering, injustice, pain, and closed doors are real. In the beginning we were declared good, and that goodness was based on being created by a good God.

Children need to attach to caregivers to develop and become fully human. We've all seen pictures of children in orphanages denied of what they need. Those images are heart wrenching because you and I know that humans need relationships and part of our being healthy, autonomous beings involves encounters with outside-of-ourselves relationships. In psychology this process is called *earned secure attachment*; in theological terms it's described as union with Christ. In children, secure attachment for babies opens a door to a whole host of positive ways of interacting with the world. Though the information I'm about to share may seem simple and obvious, read through it with the lens of how attachment allows a child to experience goodness. When a child has a secure attachment, they're able to separate from their parents, seek comfort when scared, they show positive emotions when meeting after separation, and they prefer to be with their parents rather than a stranger. People who have developed a secure attachment to a caregiver tend to have high self-esteem, enjoy long-lasting relationships, and feel comfortable sharing their emotions.[21] Consider the benefits when secure attachment is present, and think of how much you and I, as adults, also need to be attached to Someone greater than ourselves. Secure attachment to God allows us to weather separation from God, both perceived and real. Even on the cross, Christ called out, "My God, my God, why have you forsaken me?" (Matthew 27:46). It also helps us turn to God for comfort and show positive emotions when we are comforted, trusting in God's goodness.

When thinking about attachment, I can romanticize the process and picture a new mother rocking her infant, surrounded by beautiful books, clean toys, and chirping birds. But more often, attachment looks like a visit to an orphanage I had. I was visiting a group of teachers in Northeast China who served in the same organization I did. Every Saturday some of the adults and children on the team took college students to the local orphanage to play with the orphans for a couple of hours. The older orphanage kids spent the time outside playing catch, running around, and exploring the playground equipment with the foreigners and Chinese college students. The facility also had a "baby" room with infants who weren't walking yet, so some of us spent time holding babies. The toddlers lived on the same floor with the babies, and on the day I visited, we kept them inside to hold and play with instead of bundling them up to go outside.

I spent most of my time with the toddlers. My colleagues wore what they called their "orphanage pants" because they knew that they would be urinated on, touched with gooey hands, and smeared with mucus from runny noses. I didn't know about bringing orphanage pants and had packed lightly, so I didn't have a lot of clothes to change into. This might be the time to tell you that I am not really into bodily fluids. Okay, they gross me out. So, there I was in the toddler room trying to avoid bodily fluids and about to get a master class in attachment needs from the best teachers in the world: toddlers. The first lesson was that these kids know their needs and were not afraid to demand them. They wanted snacks and to be held . . . and not always in that order. When we entered the room, the toddlers ran to us with their arms up. What a picture it was! They were craving touch. The caregivers were kind and attentive, and the conditions were decent; it's just that number of kids exceeded the number of caregivers, and they simply didn't have time to hold all of the kids as much as they needed to be held throughout the course of each day.

I can't refrain from stating the obvious: toddlers with snacks are gooey messes. I tried to hold them without risking getting a gooey hand on me. Yeah right! I also tried sitting on the ground so that I could hold more on my lap and offer physical touch to as many as possible at one time. *No doing, lady! Stand up and hold us!!! Oh, and could we have more snacks so that we can goo you some more?* I have a picture from that visit in which I'm holding a little girl who was in the process of being adopted. Her pickup date had been pushed back several times, and her new family was anxious to hold her. As I held her, I kept thinking of how I was holding her until they could.

God is not like me in this scenario because He doesn't have to wear special pants in preparation to spend time with me and He doesn't try to maximize touch while minimizing the gooey mess. Yet this is probably a more realistic picture of attachment conditions when people, apart from God, are scrambling to get their needs met elsewhere: multiple people clamoring for a limited number of resources, with oozing or drooling mixed in. These experiences can birth scarcity thinking and reacting, rather than responding, because they're trying to attach to something that will end or run out. Instead, God walks in with all the time, all the snacks, all the lap space, and invites His children to connect to Him. When we are attached to God, He is the source of our goodness.

Psalm 1 describes the blessed as being "like a tree planted by streams of water," able to bear fruit in season (Psalm 1:3). Goodness is the final fruit in the second triad, which focuses on our relationships with others. We've explored patience and kindness when it comes to interacting with others; goodness rounds out the ways that God will equip you to be like that tree planted by streams of water, able to bear fruit in your interactions with others.

A QUESTION GOODNESS WHISPERS

On the surface, this is the fruit most cross-cultural workers easily envision pre-field. Before moving to the field, you build a support team by casting a vision of the good you will do. Which makes sense! If you don't know why you are going to the field and how you plan to participate in the Great Commission, I'm not sure you should be going. Of course, on your way to the field or once you arrive, God may redirect you in an unexpected way, and you may end up doing something different than you thought you'd be doing. But my point is that before you arrive, you might have pictured yourself doing a specific kind of good. In my case, I was a trained teacher who was drawn to the need for native English speakers in China. I saw a clear need where my unique gifts could help both Chinese society and the kingdom of God. Whether you're doing something that is similarly practical or perhaps more spiritual on the surface—church planting or Bible translation—you've probably pictured yourself doing good in the field.

Even if you read books like *When Helping Hurts* after arriving on the field, you might have had to consider the "good" you were doing. For me, when I thought about the English skills I was helping to develop, I was proud and could see the difference in my students' abilities after their two years at the school where I taught. My students were junior and senior high school English teachers who would use their improved skills in both English and teaching methodology when they returned to their countryside schools. I was helping the helpers! And sharing my faith in appropriate ways.

I'll be honest, though: the lack of apparent spiritual fruit year after year, when many of my colleagues in other areas of the same country had "amazing" stories, grew disheartening. Still, I could console myself that I *was* doing good by lovingly investing in my students. Until. Until the day I ran into a former student who was back in Chengdu on a work trip. I remember it vividly. His English skills had regressed so much we could barely have a conversation in English. Friend, I was so discouraged. Yes, we were in China, and since he had left teaching, he probably didn't need English skills. But walking away from him, I questioned my work. Why was I pouring my whole self into teaching? In that moment it felt like a wave had washed up and erased years of lesson planning, showing up early for class, and going the extra mile. I imagine you've had similar experiences. At some point something you've invested in hasn't stood the test of time, and you, too, have felt discouraged.

As I continued walking home, questioning if I was making any difference in the world, the quiet voice of God asked, "Are you investing in English or in people? While the English skills may fade, the way you made him feel with your kindness and faithfulness will last, and those feelings will point to me."

Something in me released with this gentle reminder. At the same time, and I am not proud of this, I felt a "But God!" rise within me. "But God, I want my work and the ways I invest my time to be more permanent than that!" If you feel something similar reading this, I don't think we are wrong to feel this way. If everything we invest in can just disappear, what's the point? Goodness calls us to manage the tension of the temporary nature of our work *and* its lasting nature. If we were in person discussing the nature of our work—both yours and mine—I think we'd easily agree that people are the most important part of our work. Yes, clean water, good education, adequate medical care, Bible translation, at-risk youth programs, work options for those coming out of trafficking, and the many other avenues for the good news of the gospel to set people free—they all matter. But they matter *because of* the people they impact, the hope they offer, and the freedom they make possible. It is important to recognize the harm we may do and the assumptions we make that could be, at best, naive and, at worst, destructive. Goodness is humble and strong enough to handle the weight of these problems because it manifests the ways God wants to bless and benefit His children. The gift of goodness is that it helps us manage the tensions that come up when we think of the harm or the permanence of what we do with the quiet question, "Are you investing in projects or people?"

GOODNESS AND ROCKY SOIL

Let's pause in our discussion of goodness and remind ourselves that God came to set the captives free! What does freedom look like? A life flowing with the fruit of the Spirit, not a life without problems. Recall earlier when we talked about Paul's letter to the Galatians. He was frustrated by ways they had inadvertently traded freedom for rules, rules that they thought would make them happy and free. God's idea of freedom is rich and comprehensive because we don't have to pick and choose between the nine fruit. Instead, all nine can flow through us simultaneously, interacting and supporting each other. In the first section of this book we looked at the freedom we embody that points us to God as the source of our love, joy, and peace. The next grouping of freedoms that this section covers is seen in our interactions with each other: patience, kindness, and goodness. Ironically, like grapes bearing fruit in rocky soil, they are more likely to spring to life in more challenging situations.

You've probably heard that the main reason people leave the field is because of the challenges of working with fellow Christians. Whether this is in fact true or more of an urban myth, we can agree there are elements of truth to it. I'm sure you've encountered people and wondered, "How did you get through screening?" One year, to save money, my organization did not use professional psychological screening. Let's just say, we never made that mistake again!

Moving to the field, you know that you need to make accommodations and that it will take time to adjust to your new environment. Before I went to the field, I naively assumed that people within my organization would get along because we were all Christians called by God to a common task. Wrong. Well, that's not entirely fair. It's true that we loved Jesus and shared the desire to see more people come to know Him and grow in their relationship with Him. But the surface areas where we differed seemed greater than what we had in common. How much time should a person give to language study? What can you do to rest? What does the Sabbath look like? How often should you talk to people back home? While all of these questions have merit, they also have something else in common. Taken one way, they are life-giving questions that help you live well in the land where God has called you to live. But examined from another angle, they're veiled attempts at defining what could be seen as "the law à la cross-cultural work."

Enter goodness, who embodies kindness that springs from generosity toward our fellow workers. My organization had a drinking policy, and as part of the organization we all agreed not to partake of alcohol while in our region of the world. Like many organizations, people new to the organization signed a policy document as part of joining the organization. The document was pages long and contained mostly policies that fall in the "Duh!

Isn't that a given?" or "I have no problem signing because it's already a part of my life" category. (Case in point: I will not use illegal drugs.) Since you too have sat around talking with fellow cross-cultural workers, it will be no surprise that more air time was given to the drinking policy than any other. For some cultures where alcohol is woven in to the culture, the types of discussions North Americans have—oh, say, since America tried to ban all alcohol as a country and that ended up being a horrible social experiment—can veer into the absurd quickly.

Why am I talking about an alcohol policy when it comes to goodness and working together? Not because we all could use a drink, but because this is where goodness is needed. Not on the large-scale big vision we can easily agree on, but here in the small, daily grind of life, where I might disagree with your take on a policy and you might disagree with mine. Years ago, Beth (who was not actually named Beth) started to experience unbearable hot flashes that interfered with her sleep. Her apartment bordered a noisy street that was already the bane of her existence. After years of living in Tibet, the powers that be hadn't granted her a work permit. Moving from a quieter, starkly beautiful city to a loud and bustling city had not been her idea of an easy "Yes, Lord! I will go where you call!" So, hot flashes on top of transition and street noise almost pushed her over the edge.

As the head of the member care department, I was the enforcer of policy on the field. Her member care person called me after visiting Beth and said, "Amy, I've been doing some internet research and have an idea of how we can help Beth." I think it's obvious, but since we are in the middle of a discussion about policies and interpretation, I am not a doctor (or a nurse or anything remotely medical), and what I'm about to share is not medical advice or a loophole for you and your own organization's policies . . . even though it might be good news for some of you! He went on to share that he'd read about the benefits of drinking one beer a day for women who struggle with hot flashes and wondered what I thought about making a policy exception for Beth. My first thought was, *I think I'm going to be more on board with this than Beth will be.*

Beth became the only person I know who was given permission to consume a beer a day for a season in her life. We talked with her and worked together to find a way to adhere to the intention behind the policy. Goodness invites us to look below the surface. I chose this example because of the universality of it. As Jesus said (and I paraphrase), "If you love those who agree with you on a policy, what credit is that to you? Even sinners love those who agree with them. And if you do good to those who are good to you, what credit is that to you? Even sinners do that" (see Luke 6:32–33). People are wired to do good to each other, but in our fallen, limited, broken ways we too often default to doing good only toward those to whom it's easy to do to good.

One of the ways doing good to all, friends and enemies, can be confusing is that Jesus redefines our relationships with each other and calls us family. Later in his letter to the Galatians, after writing about the life of flesh and the life of the Spirit, Paul says, "Therefore, as we have opportunity, let us do good to all people, especially to those who belong to the family of believers" (Galatians 6:10). We, you and I and your annoying teammate and your clueless organization, we're a part of the family of believers who are supposed to watch out for each other and do good to each other.

What I have noticed in myself is that, more than any other of the fruit, goodness asks me, "Where's your focus?" When my focus is on others with more of a slide glance to God, doing good involves my will. While there *is* a place for self-control—keep reading!—buckling down and doing good because it's what I'm "supposed to do" isn't very freeing. But when I reverse positions and focus on God with a side glance to others, goodness is more likely to flow from God through me.

So, what are we to do with teammates who truly shouldn't be on the field? For instance, someone experiencing either mental illness to the point they can't function, an anger problem that involves shoving, or blatant disregard for local norms or organizational policies? Unfortunately, the default too often is to ignore these problems, hoping they go away. In some cases, the approach that says "We're all Christians, so let's ignore it and trust God" works. But often, this approach causes more damage than it should in a situation. When I was head of member care, one of my litmus tests was "Is it more loving to address this? Or is it more loving to ignore it?" Which is a very different question than "Do I want to have this conversation?" Goodness seeks the generous life for all people, even difficult ones.

The text simply said, "Can we talk?" I wanted to reply, "No, because yesterday I said all that I wanted to say. I told you that your wife's treatment of your teammate is unacceptable and you have three weeks to leave the field. I gave you a clear end date with our organization and parameters for the ways you can interact with others from our organization in your city until that date. I do not want to rehash the whys of this decision."

But it was the first interaction I'd had with them where they asked a question—ever. Normally in this couple's interactions with me, they'd tell me (1) why they knew everything, (2) God was amazing and had told them they were right, and (3) everyone else did not know as much as they did. Adding to the complexity of the situation, they had recently relocated from one country of service within our organization to China—a move, I felt, had been made to pass the buck of dealing with difficult people. Our organization wasn't above reproach in this situation. While it was easier to pass them along, it wasn't more loving (certainly not to me in that moment!).

So when I received their text, everything in me wanted to say, "No!!!" but I replied, "Yes. I'm free now."

The following hour was holy ground. We briefly covered the behavior that had been unacceptable, and then out of the blue the husband blurted out, "We need help. Will you help us?" Later his wife told me that she was shocked when those words came tumbling out. It turns out, though they had been in full-time ministry for decades, this wasn't the first significant rupture they'd experienced. Sadly, it was the first time someone had explained to them why their actions were unacceptable. When I heard their story of being kicked out of a denomination and then crashing and burning after years of service on another continent, I wondered how they got through our organization's good screening process.

But more so, I was saddened that ample bread crumbs in their story had been repeatedly overlooked because, in this case, the wife spoke with "the authority of Christ" ... if Christ were a self-righteous bully. She wasn't easy to confront, even for me when I was trained to have these kinds of conversations! False goodness is easier in the moment, but like false gold, it has little lasting value. True goodness seeks kind generosity. In a surprise plot twist for all involved, we worked out that they could extend their time with the organization to include a month-long stay—that extended to three months—at an intensive counseling center for cross-cultural workers; this allowed them access to insurance and a way for their supporters to financially support them.

In the end, praise God, they are changed people.

Goodness doesn't turn a blind eye or have to put on rosy glasses. Instead, rooted in God's generous kindness, true goodness is able to step into messy, complex situations and sit beside patience and kindness.

In the next section, we'll turn to the final three fruit, and these three focus on one of your favorite people: you.

LET US PRAY

Grant me, O Lord, for your sake, through the work of your Holy Spirit, love for those I've come to serve and those I serve with, joy in the midst of the mundane and the miraculous of my life, and peace that starts within me and flows to others.

Add to these fruit that flow from You patience, that I may be long-tempered with those I interact with today, kindness that is useful to them and life-giving to me, and goodness that moves me to action. Amen.

INWARD

FAITHFULNESS

GENTLENESS

SELF-CONTROL

FAITHFULNESS

Whoever can be trusted with very little can also be trusted with much, and whoever is dishonest with very little will also be dishonest with much.

—Luke 16:10

I have a friend who was raised in a chaotic environment and has worked faithfully on her mental health. At times it's a challenge for her to hold on to the changes she's made. Even after years of counseling, stacks of books, and lots of practicing of healthier thought patterns and responses, she still slips into old ways on occasion. The most common time of day for these old habits to reappear is at night when she's crawled into bed. For her, these slips manifest in a double-edged sword of "what went wrong that day" and "what could go wrong the next day." Lying in bed, she replays conversations she's had that day and worries about the disasters that await her the next day.

Whether you're like her or not, chances are you can relate to my friend because her freedom from her chaotic childhood is both hard-won *and* still worth fighting for. This is the both/and of our faith. I'm sheepish to admit that sometimes in the interactions with my friend I can sound as exasperated as Paul with the Galatians. I care for my friend and (at times) need every single fruit of the

Spirit to be actively present when we communicate.

Upward, outward, inward. I need the upward-focused fruit, as I need to remember God's love for her, God's sense of joy with the growth she's made, and His peace when mine is waning. I need the outward-focused fruit—patience, kindness, and goodness—in my interactions with her. In my most exasperated moments I want to blame every drop of my frustration on her, but the truth is I'm frustrated because her "stuff" is bouncing up against (ramming into?!!) my "stuff." If Paul were to text me in those moments, can't you just picture what he'd say? He'd probably be annoyed with me and how quick I am to trade in my freedom for exasperation. Christ died not only for freedom in our relationships with God and with others, but also so that we could experience freedom within ourselves too.

We now round the corner to our final three fruit listed in Galatians: faithfulness, gentleness, and self-control. They are grouped together due to their inward focus and the ways that each one helps us more consistently be who God wants and we want to be in this world.

Like some the other fruit, *faithfulness* in Greek is larger than one word in English and can be translated in a variety of ways. Regardless of how it is translated, *pistis* embodies the idea of being trustworthy, reliable, faithful, or of having fidelity. For good reason, the idea of faithfulness is associated with marriage in the cultures many of us hail from. But that's a bit like peeling an apple and declaring it delicious after only eating the peel. For Christians, faithfulness in marriage or friendship or parenting or any relation-ship is a result of being faithful in walking with the Holy Spirit.

I was visiting a friend who leads a weekly Bible study, so I attended the study with her. As one of the leaders, my friend would ask a question from the homework and facilitate the group answering the questions. The group was studying Proverbs, and that week's Bible passage included "lady folly" going after husbands and how important faithfulness in marriage is. I was in the unique position to be welcomed into the study because of my long-standing friendship with my friend without any expectation of participation. No surprise, the group came down strongly against anyone who would have an affair.

What no one but the leaders (and I) knew was that one of the women, whom I'll call Sally, had had an affair years before. Sally didn't say anything, and neither of the leaders tried to steer the conversation away from the topic, allowing it play out. Watching the conversation unfold, I wondered how the other women would have approached the topic if they had known how personal it was to Sally, how much she regrets the affair, and how grateful she was that her marriage survived her unfaithfulness. While no one would have become pro-affair, the knowledge might have moved the conversation from being about "people out there" to "one of us" in a humanizing way.

You've probably had your own experience where you knew something other people didn't or later you found out something that would have influenced your tone or word choice. Those conversations can be awkward with a capital A. But they have a way of moving a topic from "out there" to "in here." And isn't that what Jesus did again and again? He took a subject and made it personal, showing how important it is for our external behavior to be congruent with our internal thoughts and beliefs.

YOUR SOUL HAS THREE GUARDS

In their book *Boundaries for Your Soul* authors Alison Cook and Kimberly Miller present a model based on the research of Richard C. Schwartz. Schwartz noticed that people talk about themselves in terms of "parts."[22] Schwartz wasn't the first to talk about people this way. The apostle Paul, in his letter to the Romans, said he didn't do the things he wanted to do, and instead did the things he didn't want to do (Romans 7:15). Parts of himself were not always working together. Cook and Miller say, "The goal, however, is not to get rid of your soul's parts—which would be impossible anyway—but to help them heal, grow, and discover their valuable, God-given roles."[23]

While we might seek out thrills, we don't go into a relationship or experience thinking, *I can't wait to have my heart broken, my hopes dashed, or my expectations shattered in every imaginable way.* People, no surprise, like to avoid pain. Parts of our souls have developed ways to help us avoid pain. What I found interesting in *Boundaries for Your Soul* is that the way we seek to avoid pain falls in three categories that line up with the three fruit in the inward triad. These "soul protectors" are on guard when they sense that you might be at risk of being hurt. The guards fall into three categories; managers, exiles, and firefighters.

While each one is trying to be helpful, they are getting in the way of a particular fruit coming to full maturity in us. Loosely, managers are trying to be faithful, but they can be more like meddling relatives. Exiles have confused gentleness with not engaging. And firefighters don't trust self-control to get the job done, so they run around leaving a path of chaos.

As Cook and Miller say, "When a protector takes over, however, you're no longer living from the [Holy] Spirit-led place within, and you've lost your sense of perspective."[24] I keep returning to the basics because I need the reminder: the fruit of the Spirit is not simply so I look good to the culture and people God has called me to serve; the fruit of the Spirit truly is for my freedom! Freedom that is firmly planted in reality. Which leads me to another fact I need to remind myself: grapes grow in rocky soil. God knows the challenges you face now and those you faced in the past, and He offers freedom in their midst. In this final section of the book we will add to the mix of freedom (from the first section) and reality (the second section), this idea of soul protectors, or meddling guards, that we need to ask to stand down.

The "managers" of your soul try to anticipate what could go wrong. They strive to keep you safe emotionally and prevent you from experiencing harm. On the surface this is good, but taken to an extreme it ends up isolating you more than helping you. We all need to grow in discernment because soul managers can masquerade as faithfulness when they "drive you to perform, produce, protect, and please."[25] The manager of your soul believes that getting bogged down with emotional pain is impractical, so they will just keep you moving to avoid being bogged down at all costs. This sounds like faithfulness, right? Keep moving, keep focused on the task, keep doing.

You might think,

- I'll put in long hours because Jesus is worth it.
- My family will understand because souls are at risk.
- This is simply part of the cost.
- The Lord will restore the years the locust has stolen.

Any of these could be absolutely true. Or they could completely miss the mark. Jesus is known for moving many a conversation inward. Remember the whole log/speck conversation? It reminds me of learning to shoot a bow and arrow at summer camp and how the point value increased the closer my arrow was to hitting the bull's-eye. While any point earned by hitting the target is a point earned, Jesus is metaphorically pushing us beyond thinking that we only get points for our behavior. He's broadening the target, so to speak, to less tangible parts of us, like our motivations. Look at the progression in Ephesians 2:19–20. Paul writes, "Consequently, you are no longer foreigners and strangers, but fellow citizens with God's people and also members of his household, built on the foundation of the apostles and prophets, with Christ Jesus himself as the chief cornerstone."

Notice the movement individuals can go through from being foreigners and strangers to being citizens to becoming members of the same household. It looks a bit like this: foreigners –> citizens –> family. As you mature in Christ you can experience a similar movement. What seemed foreign to you before you became a Christian grows more familiar the longer you walk with the Spirit. Since we're talking about faithfulness, on the surface being faithful or reliable seems to be about our interactions with others. For instance, if we make a commitment, we should honor it. But faithfulness is about so much more than honoring commitments.

Even as I work on this chapter, most of me is focused on you and this conversation we are having. But if I'm honest, about five percent of me is annoyed with a person I'm supposed to meet later this afternoon. I am on the board of a local ministry, and one of the staff asked if I could meet for coffee this afternoon to discuss an upcoming fundraising event. I said, "Sure!" because I do want to help and my schedule is flexible this afternoon. But she hasn't gotten back to me since our email interaction yesterday, and I'm annoyed.

It's true that my schedule is flexible and I want to help, but it's also true that I have other commitments on my schedule today as well, and at this point what I really want is to get our time nailed down so I know what my afternoon looks like. If you must know, I wanted to end the previous sentence with about seven exclamation points to depict more accurately what my inside thinks of this situation.

Right now, the manager of my soul is whisper-shouting, *People are so annoying! They don't act in efficient ways, and it always ends up costing me!*

My manager knows that I love efficiency and not being inconvenienced. Your manager will know what you love. Maybe efficiency isn't all that important to your deeply held values. Here's the thing about my deep insides: most people would have no idea how much I value efficiency because my manager also values people *not* thinking I'm a colossal jerk as I shove my way to the front of a line. Deep inside you, your soul manager might whisper that others don't see all that you have to offer. Or she might remind you that people would be in a world of hurt without you. Whatever the message is, notice how your manager may be trying to protect you in some way, which actually interferes with Jesus's invitation to dive further into the heart of a given situation.

While it still might be borderline rude not to nail down a time with me, God's been showing me, as I've been working on this section, that faithfulness is important in the big *and* the small. Yes, faithfulness is important in a marriage, to a ministry team, or to financial responsibility for the long haul. But it's also about these daily moments. Am I going to be faithful in how I think about the staff person who has also become a friend as we've worked together? Am I going to be trustworthy in my heart to be aware of my frustration without feeding it?

Being faithful doesn't mean that you or I can't be annoyed or disappointed or hurt, but it does mean that we are able to name what is going on inside us. It also means that if I'm faithful to my relationship with this person, I'm willing to own my part. Ugh. I want it all to be *her* fault for not getting back with me. When I turn from looking at her and instead look at my part, I realize I never said that I wanted to nail down a time or gave any parameters. Instead, I communicated that I'm flexible this afternoon and to let me know what works. Since it matters to me more than I realized, in the future I need to be more trustworthy in my communication with her. I could either communicate more clearly that I need to know when we will meet or, if I say I'm flexible, then I need to be flexible in my heart too.

I hope it's obvious, but since this book is being read in many different cultural contexts, let me say clearly that both the staff I'm scheduled to meet with today and I are in a culture that is time oriented. So, while the minutiae of what's going on in my soul as it relates to time might be tedious and not culturally applicable where you are, being aware of time is relevant to me. But that's kind of the point. Jesus takes these aspects of culture—time orientation, power distance, individualism/collectivism—and moves them beyond the surface. Which is both good *and* complex, isn't it? If we stay at the surface on any one of the aspects of culture, I can find loopholes why something might not apply to me. For those of us who have incorporated multiple cultures into our lives, we can too easily give ourselves a "get out of jail free" card. The China-part of Amy can operate according to very different rules than the American-part.

But superseding the China-part or the American-part of me is the Christ-follower part. The part that says, "Faithfulness is not merely about actions. It's also about attitude."

YOUR PART IN THE MOSAIC

It started off innocently enough—if I had known all that was coming, I might have tried to get my own attention and madly waved myself off. Henri Nouwen compared community to a mosaic, adding that community is not simple or easy.[26] He wasn't kidding.

It was springtime, and I mentioned to one of my colleagues in the Beijing office that I was near the end of the current season of *The Biggest Loser*. My colleague Janice said that in the fall we'd have to watch the next season together when I was in town. The spring and fall were heavy travel times for my job in member care, so having a relatively meaningless show to watch and someone to watch it with sounded delightful. And it was! Janice and I huddled around my computer in the days when "streaming" wasn't really a thing yet and we used a VPN to watch on the network. While the commercials were super annoying, they gave us time to discuss the show. I'm pretty good with names, so it was funny to find out that Janice isn't and can only remember people by the nicknames she gives them. We lived and worked in a communal setting, and when I love something, I love to talk about it (much to the annoyance of my sisters when we were in high school). So, no surprise, our discussions of *The Biggest Loser* began to flavor our conversations and interactions with others.

My neighbor Mikkin's husband was out of town in December, and Mikkin started watching *The Biggest Loser* by herself to fill the evening after she put her little one to bed. When we would run into her in the halls or on the stairwell of our communal building, we'd discuss what had happened in the most recent episode. And like that, a small community was born.

By the spring, when the next season aired, we discovered that four of us—because, of course, Mikkin's husband, Karl, wanted in on the fun—huddling around one computer wasn't an enjoyable viewing experience. Thus, I was "forced" to figure out a more enjoyable viewing option by consulting a technology expert to solve this problem: a teenager. She kindly explained the finer points of downloading. Because neither streaming nor easy downloading were yet a thing, it often took hours. But it was worth it to transfer the downloaded episode onto a thumb drive and watch it on a TV.

What started out as a casual "whenever Janice and I were both in town" viewing evolved into meeting "every Friday evening at 7:00 p.m. in the conference room" of our joint office. And word spread. Soon we were joined by others, and our community grew, and rituals like popcorn made by Karl became a given. On "makeover week" of the show we had a potluck composed of only healthy foods. For the finale we had red velvet cupcakes.

The next fall, we continued watching once the new season started, and I became the unofficial leader of our weekly viewing parties. At times I wondered, *How did this go from me watching alone to being the leader of this community?!* That fall the internet was so pesky that I spent more time than I wanted on Thursdays and Fridays getting ready for 7:00 p.m. when BLT met (Biggest Loser Team, and yes, we now had a name). Faithfulness and fussing can coexist. Weekly, and sometimes hourly, on those Thursdays or Fridays, I would mutter, "That's it. I'm done! I do *not* want to be a slave to this weekly albatross! Why does my piece of the mosaic of community involve the internet, something so time-consuming and unreliable?!"

I share so much detail here because this is often what faithfulness is: a long obedience in the same direction toward a greater good that may cost you. I'd fuss when I was alone in my apartment doing battle with the internet. But when we gathered, I was reminded that faithfulness, relationships, and community are not simple and easy, but they can be beautiful. One Friday night a loyal member of the BLT brought all the guests from his eleven-year-old birthday party. As they lay on the floor cheering for the black team, Nate looked up at me and beamed. His mom emailed me afterward to share how excited he was that "his friends were so into the show." The excitement went both ways as we got to enjoy his birthday cake during an intermission break! After that, every Monday morning he updated his TCK classmates about what had happened on the Friday night episode.

Because we watched in our organization's headquarters, anyone who was in town was welcome. Pregnant women waiting to give birth, family members visiting from distant lands who had spent the day touring, people in town for medical appointments or embassy runs, all joined in, even if only for a week or two. We continued gathering for several years, sharing births, birthday parties, illnesses, deaths, and disappointments. I started this section off referring to a Henri Nouwen quote about the mosaic of community from his book *Can You Drink the Cup?* What he wrote formed the way I think about community:

> Community is like a large mosaic. Each little piece seems
> so insignificant. One piece is bright red, another cold blue
> or dull green, another warm purple, another sharp yellow,
> another shining gold. Some look precious, others ordinary.
> Some look valuable, others worthless. Some look gaudy,

others delicate. As individual stones, we can do little with them except compare them and judge their beauty and value. When, however, all these little stones are brought together in one big mosaic portraying the face of Christ, who would ever question the importance of any one of them? If one of them, even the least spectacular one, is missing, the face is incomplete. Together in the one mosaic, each little stone is indispensable and makes a unique contribution to the glory of God. That's community, a fellowship of little people who together make God visible in the world.[27]

The same could be said of faithfulness. Each little piece, each little act or decision, seems insignificant, but together they contribute to a life that's congruent. Faithful acts, in small and large ways, each inform and form you toward the type of person you want to be and the ways you help the kingdom of God to exist here on Earth.

FAITHFULNESS TOLD IN THREE PARABLES

I love the book-writing process because of the surprises each chapter holds. As I've been working on this one, three little vignettes have followed me around my non-writing part of the day. I say "followed" when what might be a more accurate depiction is "hounded," because they insist that they *must* be part of this chapter. These stories will be glad to know that today is the day, and I will capture them here on the page for you now.

VIGNETTE 1: Faithfulness is like a cheerful customs official who has taken an oath to protect the land she serves. After a long and exhausting trip, she greets those who step up to her counter with eye contact and asks about their trip. She's been charged with the dual job of processing entrances and protecting against threats, both duties she takes seriously. Those who will benefit and enjoy the country she serves are welcome, while those who seek to do ill are not. She arrives to work on time, doesn't cut corners, and gives all who step up to her counter their due attention. The land is safe because of her.

VIGNETTE 2: Faithfulness is like a symphony made up of sections composed of multiple instruments. The instruments work together for the sake of the piece of music set before them. Not all instruments will play at the same time, so they watch the conductor and come in when cued. Faithfulness trusts in the power of many smaller sounds working together over the course of the piece of music to create something larger than any one player or sound. The standing ovation she receives is because the many became one.

VIGNETTE 3: Faithfulness is like Chinese *xiaochi* (shao-chir) or tapas first enjoyed by a foreigner. Seeing three little bowls set before him, he might wonder if he'll go home hungry. But as the meal goes on, the second wave of three little bowls, and then the third and fourth and even fifth waves of little bowls, are brought out by the server. The little bowls of food individually don't look like much. Over the course of the meal, bowl by bowl they make a meal, even a feast, leaving a guest satisfied.

Each parable highlights an aspect of faithfulness. Customs officers might not have the most glamourous job, but what they do is vital to a country. Faithfulness that cheerfully shows up day after day, like that customs official, provides for the greater good. In truth, she impacts people she'll never know and who will never know her. The image of a symphony highlights timing and volume. There are times when being faithful to our host culture is the primary sound and other times when being faithful to a relationship or obligation or a policy we signed needs to be heard. Often two or more sections will be playing at the same time. We're not simply "faithful" or "unfaithful."

And the idea of faithfulness being like xiaochi struck me because of how easy faithfulness can be to miss or misunderstand. When I first moved to China and was introduced to xiaochi, I was told it was like a snack. The literal translation is "little food," and it's true that a snack is a "little food." But I failed to grasp one key difference between xiaochi and a snack until I ate it and was so full I wanted to throw up. One is a meal, the other is not. In my first time enjoying xiaochi with Chinese friends, the waitress brought three small bowls for each of us. We ate them, and then she replaced with three more bowls of little yummy delights. Not understanding that this was going to go on for at least five rounds, I did not pace myself and ate all the contents in every bowl. By itself, one act of faithfulness may not look like much, but as the proverbial meal goes on, trust me, it adds up!

Luke 16:10 captures the heart of faithfulness: "Whoever can be trusted with very little can also be trusted with much, and whoever is dishonest with very little will also be dishonest with much." The starting place for faithfulness is to have an accurate picture of who God is. That might be a simple sentence to write and to read, but if we pause for a moment and create space to notice a bit of the God we love and serve, we need to hold his holiness, compassion, long-suffering, just, and covenantal nature all in that same space. And those attributes are just a start! It's not about understanding all of them perfectly, but you can see how, if your view of God's holiness is off, that will influence who you are faithful to and how you are faithful.

Faithfulness ripples from God, to us, and then to others. If you're faithful to your beliefs, convictions, and values, that will play out in how you're faithful to others. The good news is that faithfulness is not about white-knuckled attempts at success, isolated from the other fruit of the Spirit. With the hope of freedom and the reality of thorns, let's keep going and add gentleness to our discussion.

LET US PRAY

Grant me, O Lord, for your sake, through the work of your Holy Spirit, love for those I've come to serve and those I serve with, joy in the midst of the mundane and the miraculous of my life, and peace that starts within me and flows to others.

Add to these fruit that flow from You patience, that I may be long-tempered with those I interact with today, kindness that is useful to them and life-giving to me, and goodness that moves me to action.

Help me to be consistently moving toward the person you want me to be as I am faithful in word and deed. Amen.

GENTLENESS

A gentle answer turns away wrath,
but a harsh word stirs up anger.
—Proverbs 15:1

'm a little surprised how often my elbows are referenced in my newsletters, personal correspondence, and blog posts. I even entitled one blog post "I Want to Blame China, but They Are My Elbows."[28] In the post I recounted flying from Beijing to Cambodia via Seoul and described my approach to boarding as being in "game on travel mode!" Right there that description should be code for needing more gentleness. Elbows out, I approached boarding the plane as if I were a defensive lineman and I was trying to take out anyone in my path.

Plopping in my seat, I reflected for a bit on my less-than-gentle approach. A bit too quickly, my thinking went to, "Well, that's life in China." Public transportation requires a certain amount of aggressiveness or you'll never get on the subway, exit a bus, or hail a taxi.

If I had a nickel for every time over the years I heard, "When in Rome, do as the Romans," in reference to being sensitive in cross-cultural service, I would never need to pay for public transportation again. Of course, we need to adjust to our host environments. What I'm getting at isn't about transportation; it's about how I shifted the blame and justified to myself that because of the context my unnecessarily aggressive approach was excusable, even justifiable.

Here's what I texted a friend: "I want to blame China, but they're my elbows."

Sigh. Once again, Jesus shows how the discussion isn't "out there" as much as it is "in here." I need this second, inwardly focused fruit of gentleness because without it my knee-jerk reaction is to focus on the external and give myself a pass. Thankfully, more good news is nestled in fruit of gentleness: it's so much more than tone and elbows.

Elbows, however, seem to be the messenger God uses to tangibly remind me of my need for this fruit in my life. As you know, sometimes transitioning from one culture to another goes smoothly and other times . . . what's the opposite of smooth and gentle? Rocky and violent? Yeah, like that. On another plane, this time from Thailand to Beijing, I noticed it was harder for me as an American living in China to transition from Thailand to China than from America to China.

Part of it was the time of year I tended to make transitions. I eagerly anticipated my trips to Thailand for an annual work meeting in February for many reasons. But flowers, blue skies, and warm weather sure helped! Aesthetically speaking, returning from colorful and warm Thailand back to Beijing, which in February looks washed out, was part of my culture-transition problem. But I also think that for me, transitioning between America and China, my head had an internal switch that I flipped because the two cultures were so different. In going from Thailand to China, I forgot to flip the switch and just thought, *Oh, it's Asia, same-same* . . . when it's not.

On that particular flight, as a teammate and I boarded the plane with mostly Chinese passengers, I felt my crankiness level rising. *Why is everyone shoving? Hello, ma'am, could you please remove your nose from my back?* I felt a surge of aggressiveness. After being in the "land of smiles," as Thailand is nicknamed, it was a shock to be returning to the "land of the elbows." Jostled in the shoving herd, a paper my student wrote the previous spring came to mind. At that point in my teaching career I taught very high level graduate students at one of the top universities in China. They were in an elite program and very likely destined to work in the government in the future. In the spring semester we'd studied a unit on the values and beliefs of Americans so that the students could understand the behavior of Americans. Often the automatic reaction from my students was, "Why is the US government *always* doing [xyz] *to us?*" If ever a need for gentleness existed, it is in trying to understand why a culture does something that is unfamiliar and confusing, am I right? In class we would discuss how certain American behaviors, especially of the American government, often aren't personal; instead, they flow (hopefully) out of the values and beliefs of American culture.

As part of the unit, we read an article entitled "The Waiting Game."[29] I remember it because the article was an insightful discussion of what helps Americans to wait more patiently. It even helped me understand myself more! The article argued that certain factors, such as having information on how long the wait will be, knowing whether or not there is a delay and the reason for it, or having something to do during the wait (like read), all help with waiting. It used Disneyland as an example of a business that had perfected the art of waiting by snaking lines and providing entertainment during the wait.

At the tail end of the article, the author briefly mentioned that part of waiting is mostly cultural conditioning and gave examples from different cultures. Well, there was one sentence about China and good golly if it didn't push my students' buttons, and I understood why. I've had my buttons pushed plenty of times by something said about America that I disagreed with. At the end of our discussion, I asked if anyone had any questions, and the entire class wanted to know if I agreed with the perceptions of the author. Yikes.

I delicately explained that I could understand what the author was saying, but she probably had been traveling at the Spring Festival time, and we all know that is the craziest travel time. I added that when I board busses, I don't like that I have to use my elbows to shove on and off. I gently continued that I didn't fully understand why people waiting to board the subway didn't let the passengers get off the subway before they try to get on. On cultural cue, the students pointed out the large population in China. I agreed that it was true the population is large, but I tried to point out, lovingly, that Seoul, Korea, also has a large population without a shove-fest when boarding the subway. Hong Kong, New York City, Paris, London, all of these cities also have large populations. So population isn't the only factor.

"Oh," they corporately sighed and admitted, "You're right."

IT'S NOT JUST MY ELBOWS

Of all the articles and topics we explored, it was the article about waiting that stayed with them. At the end of the term students were assigned to choose one of the areas we had looked at and write a paper. I'm going to share part of one student's paper because it illustrates the process we all go through when the Holy Spirit points out an area that needs addressing. She's not a Christian, which means we won't get lost in any cleaned-up Christian language—you know the kind I'm talking about, the kind only "seasoned" Christians tend to use—and truly see the process.

As an arts student, I am quite interested in learning about different cultures. However, after reading "The Waiting Game," I am shocked by the sentence in the article 'In China, though it is sometimes not a line but mass hysteria. At some train stations, people don't just push to the front of the line—they actually climb over the people in front of them.' Amy, you are right, as a Chinese, I do not agree with the description in the article at first, I often think the author does not understand China much, and even never came to China. She exaggerated and has some prejudice to east countries. So these days, I observe the people around, chat with my foreign friends, and discuss in our class in order to find something that can change the description in the article strongly; but I failed. It makes me think deeply, and feel terribly uncomfortable. Maybe this article is not a perfect paper, but it is all the true feeling of my deep heart.

Scenes of waiting in China appear in front of my eyes: There are no clear lines in the dining room in my school, everyone tries to push ahead. When I ask the boy who is cutting in front of me to wait in line, he looks at me surprised, "Why are you so fussy?" Oh my, I want to curse him to never get a girlfriend. When I draw cash from an ATM machine, the person waiting behind me is so close to me! When we are waiting for the subway, there is no line preparing for the door to open. No one remembers "out first and get on later,"

SECTION 3 - INWARD

and everyone use elbows. (Oh, Amy's poor elbows come in my mind again.) The worst place is railway station, where everyone seems to be crazy, and there are a lot of policeman who are shouting and trying to keep people in order. It always feels like finish a fight when I finally get my seat. People seldom bring books or something else when they are waiting, and I never see a place as smart as Disney that give you enough information to dispel the sense of waiting, no one will tell you how long you will need to be in line.

Yes, above are just some simple examples of waiting in China. I agree that waiting is a trivial thing in our daily life. However, is it too small to pay attention? Or can it be ignored? No, I don't think so, it is why I feel strong in the bottom of my heart. Sometimes people always ascribe it to the big population of China, however, it's only an excuse, and actually the population density of New York and Beijing is quite similar. In fact, it reflects some big problems in Chinese culture in my mind.

My student ended her paper with, "Yes, it is an order age, just like the Chinese saying, 'no order, no success.' As a confident and cultured Chinese student, I appeal to all Chinese people 'Please wait in line.'"

Though she's not a Christian, her paper is a beautiful example of what it looks like when the fruit of the Spirit is walking with someone. Instead of saying, "Look, sweety, stop being defensive," the Spirit patiently walked with a person as she began to see parts of life in a new way. He also stirred within my student the desire for kindness and goodness for the benefit of society. What I find so compelling about her paper is that she set out to prove the author (and maybe me) wrong and it took her first on an internal journey. Though she couldn't really change anything around her, in the end *she* changed. If Jesus was telling His parables today, I imagine these are the types of illustrations He would use. He'd tell about the foreigner boarding a plane with the nose of those she came to serve shoved in her back. After pausing to let the listeners reflect on the story, He might ask, "Who was truly gentle?" Like you, they'd get his point that gentleness isn't just about elbows; it's also about your heart and your thoughts.

"I DO NOT THINK IT MEANS WHAT YOU THINK IT MEANS"
In a classic scene in the movie *The Princess Bride*, the swordsman Inigo Montoya says a line, regarding the word *inconceivable*, that has become infamous: "You keep using that word. I do not think it means what you think it means." It turns out, the same could be said of the word *gentleness*.

When I think of gentleness, I see one of my nieces, when she was two years old, around a newborn. She was so excited to see the baby and wanted to hold and love on this new sister, but she didn't know her own strength and needed to be reminded, "Gentle, gentle. Be gentle with your sister." I associate gentleness with tone or use of force. *What a gentle tone she has. He has a gentle touch.*

We cross-cultural worker get how some concepts don't translate easily. *Prautes* is the Greek word that we translate in English as "gentleness." Of the nine fruit listed, gentleness is the most untranslatable, and *gentle* has three main meanings in the New Testament:

1. Submissive to the will of God
2. Teachable, as the person who is not too proud to learn
3. Most often it means considerate.[30]

Of those three meanings, probably the idea of being considerate comes closest to how we use it in English. As I studied and prepared for this book and the structure emerged with three fruit grouped with an upward focus (love, joy, and peace), three with an outward focus (patience, kindness, and goodness), and these final three with an inward focus (faithfulness, gentleness, and self-control), it was gentleness that made me scratch my head. Isn't gentleness needed most with my interactions with others?

Submissive and teachable, however, start with me. They start *in* me. Think of a well-trained pet who is quick to respond to his owner. When I was in second grade, one of my good friends was outside with her adult neighbor, other kids, and the neighbor's dog. Unprovoked, the dog bit my friend Jess on the face, severely puncturing both cheeks and requiring immediate medical attention. Until we were in high school, Jess had plastic surgery every couple of years because of the significant amount of scar tissue on her face. The dog's behavior was an absolute shock because it had never before shown any signs of aggressive behavior.

While it is impossible to say why the dog attacked my friend, it is a powerful reminder to me that true gentleness doesn't look like one thing—in this instance, a friendly neighborhood dog—and act another way. If I am truly a "tamed dog," I will know my Master's voice and submit to it. I both love and hate this! I love that the fruit of gentleness is possible for every single person and not simply for some who are "good at that kind of thing." But I hate it because now I'm accountable, and just like an animal may need to go to obedience school; you and I may need additional training not to become distracted by the squirrels of this life. Or worse, end up doing permanent damage to each other in one random moment.

Aristotle explained gentleness as the person who is so in control of themselves that they are always angry at the right time and never angry at the wrong time.[31] That is worth repeating. A gentle person is someone who is angry at the right time and never angry at the wrong time. Gentleness and anger, then, are related. Have you ever associated anger with gentleness? Probably not, but once you do, it will open you up to the depths of genuine gentleness. Because many Christians are taught that anger isn't a sign of a "good Christian," part of you will try to protect your soul from the discomfort of anger by exiling it.

Last chapter I introduced the idea that your soul has three protectors: managers, exiles, and firefighters. Each believes that it's trying to help you avoid pain, but the truth is they are hindering your maturity in some area or another. When you don't know how to point with the "sword of truth" in a situation, you have two options: hack with the sword, causing damage, or hide the sword. In the name of gentleness, exiles have confused gentleness with not engaging and often "yielded their power in counterproductive ways."[32]

Not long after I'd moved to Beijing, an American teacher had a minor bicycle accident with a local Beijing woman. The fifty-year-old woman caught her sleeve on his backpack, lost her balance, and fell over. Thankfully, she wasn't badly hurt and was able to walk around. Honestly, if you know traffic in large Asian cities, you know the bike lanes are crowded and it's more amazing if you *don't* bump into someone than if you do. But this wasn't a normal bump; this was a bump with a foreigner. You probably know where this is going. The police were summoned, the woman was taken to the hospital (where it was determined that she had a sprained ankle but nothing was broken), and the next day the teacher was questioned by the police.

Because he was in my organization, later that week I found

myself, along with my boss, the teacher, his school official, and a Chinese lawyer in a meeting. The lawyer said that if the teacher had not been a foreigner, there'd be no case. Because he wasn't in a position of social power (as an outsider) yet was perceived to be wealthy, her children had filed the case. Going into the meeting, my boss encouraged us to "focus on being righteous instead of being right." That's worth repeating too: being righteous is more important than being right.

I could rationally understand all the points of view. The accident wasn't different from thousands of accidents that happen every day. But the truth is my colleague probably did have access to more financial resources than the woman he hit. However, as a famous Chinese saying goes, "Nothing is what it seems," so the woman and her family could have been wealthy and simply taking advantage of the situation. During the meeting my feelings bounced around from annoyed at the unfairness of the situation to guilt at the inequity in the world and then over to distrust and wanting to avoid feeling like a sucker. It was an internal ping-pong match between my personal justice, systemic justice, and culture. I know, I know. That's three players, but it turns out that internal ping-pong doesn't really care about rules that govern actual games.

Ah, isn't that the nature of the internal world, revealing how some of the fruit are especially laser-focused inward? Proverbs 15:1 turns out to be an excellent litmus test for my heart and my motives: "A gentle answer turns away wrath, but a harsh word stirs up anger." When we see an injustice in the world, gentleness is angry because anger *is* the appropriate response. Instead of exiling part of yourself, sometimes gentleness acknowledges that something is wrong. When I saw one of my students being beaten by her husband on the campus of our school in Chengdu and no one did anything, I was incensed on the inside. My reaction was gentleness in action. We have been trained to think that gentleness and anger look quite different, when they don't always. I admit that the situation was complicated by the different cultural rules at play and my lack of language skills at the time. I'm not saying we don't factor in cultural considerations, but as Inigo Montoya said, "I do not think [gentleness] means what you think it means."

WAS JESUS GENTLE?

It's a familiar story. It was almost time for the Passover, so Jesus and the apostles traveled to Jerusalem. "In the temple courts he found people selling cattle, sheep and doves, and others sitting at tables exchanging money" (John 2:14). Let's pretend you don't know what comes next and I tell you Jesus responded gently to the situation, then ask you what you think He did. What would you guess He did? You might guess that Jesus looked for who was in charge or went around to each seller and money exchanger and told them a parable that cut to the heart of the issue. The parable convicted them and motivated them to change.

If I said, "Well, let's see what Jesus actually did" and continued the story, I bet you'd be surprised to hear this: "So he made a whip out of cords, and drove all from the temple courts, both sheep and cattle; he scattered the coins of the money changers and overturned their tables. To those who sold doves he said, 'Get these out of here! Stop turning my Father's house into a market!'" (John 2:15–16).

Made a whip? Yes, made a whip. Not just picked up a whip, made a whip. And then He used that whip to chase people out of the temple courts and yelled at them to stop turning His house into a "den of thieves," as Matthew's Gospel says (Matthew 21:13 KJV). This is a so-called gentle response?

Here's another familiar story that also took place in the temple courts. It was early in the morning and people had gathered around to hear Jesus teach. He'd just begun when some religious leaders interrupted and presented a woman caught in adultery. To make their point, the leaders had her stand in the midst of all who were present while they tried to trap Jesus with His interpretation of the law. Once again, let's pretend you don't know what happened, and I pause and tell you that Jesus responded gently to the situation, then ask you what you think He did. You might just shrug and say you don't know, knowing that this might also be a trap for you. I'm kidding! Sort of. Here's what Jesus did:

But Jesus bent down and started to write on the ground with his finger. When they kept on questioning him, he straightened up and said to them, "Let any one of you who is without sin be the first to throw a stone at her." Again he stooped down and wrote on the ground.

At this, those who heard began to go away one at a time, the older ones first, until only Jesus was left, with the woman still standing there. Jesus straightened up and asked her, "Woman, where are they? Has no one condemned you?"

"No one, sir," she said.

"Then neither do I condemn you," Jesus declared. "Go now and leave your life of sin." (John 8:6–11)

I have to admit, *this* is the Jesus I see as gentle. Writing in the dirt. Quietly and poignantly condemning the self-righteous leaders. The interaction concludes with a meaningful exchange with the woman. "Go and sin no more" (John 8:11 NLT). *Now, that's gentleness*, I might think. Not the whip-making, table-turning, screaming Jesus. Which Jesus do you think is gentle? Not right or effective in His actions, but gentle.

Turns out, both are.

If gentleness was more about tone or the way you interact with others, it might fit with the second group of fruit that's more outward focused, lumped together under the umbrella of interacting with others, it might fit with the second group of fruit that's more outward focused, lumped together under the umbrella of interacting with others. As a brief reminder, what fruit is born in our inter-actions? Patience, kindness, and goodness. With my limited understanding of gentleness, I might have swapped goodness with gentleness and said it fit better here, with these inward-focused fruit, and gentleness fits better with the more outward-focused fruit. But Jesus is after more than our tone of voice or use of force, isn't He? Thus, gentle Jesus made a whip because He could not stand seeing a place of worship turned into a place of commerce that took advantage of the vulnerable. He was angry at the right thing. And gentle Jesus read the situation with the woman correctly too. He knew she was a pawn in a larger "game" that wasn't about her. He saw beyond the religious leaders' question to their trap and knew that anger wasn't the best reply. I need to say it again because my brain needs to build new neural pathways between gentleness and anger. Pathways that help me be in tune with the Holy Spirit so that I get angry at the right time and avoid being angry at the wrong time.

You've probably heard people say they don't like the God of the Old Testament because He's so angry. True gentleness asks us to time our anger to God's heartbeat. If I'm honest, too often my anger is tied to what frustrates or inconveniences me, and not often enough with what breaks God's heart. As gentleness grows in you and me, our gentleness will be tethered more to God's heart and less to our own.

GENTLENESS AND CROSS-CULTURAL SERVICE

My friend and long-time colleague Joann Pittman is beloved by people in our organization for two reasons. First, she gets to teach about culture, and what do most of us find fascinating? Culture. Second, she is gifted at one-liners that carry a whole world of knowledge. One of her oft-repeated lines for life and ministry in China is "nothing is as it seems." Joann explains, "In fact, I would say this rule applies when observing and analyzing nearly all segments of life in China: politics, economy, social relationships, and even religion. To put it another way, whatever China seems to be at any given moment, it is in fact, the opposite. This can be difficult for westerners because we tend to be dichotomist in our thinking, wanting something to be either this or that. We don't do well with this AND that."[33]

God seems to be far more comfortable with *and* than we are. Gentleness is about being considerate *and* willing to be angry. It involves being teachable *and* willing to take a stand. It invites us to use our words *and* our tone in accordance with the Holy Spirit's prompting. Gentleness training may start with young children, like my nieces around babies, but it is for all of us. Earlier in this chapter I shared that the Greek word for this fruit is hard to translate and I can see how limited the English concept of gentleness is. I feel like we've been to a zoo together to see a majestic animal like a tiger, hippo, or giraffe. As amazing as those animals are to see at the zoo, it pales in comparison to seeing those animals set free in their natural habitat. So it is with gentleness. True gentleness set free within ourselves is powerful, majestic, and a bit wild.

I'm reminded of another line Joann used to say, quoting Rob Gifford: "If you're not confused, then you simply haven't been paying attention."[34] Gentleness has confused me in a good sense. If it has confused you too, that's okay. It means we're paying attention. Now to the next fruit we'll consider, and if you thought you were confused with gentleness, self-control holds its own surprises for you.

LET US PRAY

Grant me, O Lord, for your sake, through the work of your Holy Spirit, love for those I've come to serve and those I serve with, joy in the midst of the mundane and the miraculous of my life, and peace that starts within me and flows to others.

Add to these fruit that flow from You patience, that I may be long-tempered with those I interact with today, kindness that is useful to them and life-giving to me, and goodness that moves me to action.

Help me to be consistently moving toward the person you want me to be as I am faithful in word and deed and to exhibit gentleness that is always angry at the right time and never angry at the wrong time. Amen.

SELF-CONTROL

It is not good to eat too much honey, nor is it honorable to search out matters that are too deep. Like a city whose walls are broken through is a person who lacks self-control.
—Proverbs 25:27–28

My first apartment in China was owned by the Foreign Affairs Office (FAO). Every summer the FAO wanted my teammate and me to "go home" so that they could use our apartments to house teachers in a summer program. At the end of each spring semester Erin, and later Shelley, and I packed up the contents of our apartments in boxes and stored them in a corner. One summer, the rooms were repainted before we returned and air conditioning was installed. I repeat, glorious air conditioning units were installed in each room; let the heavens open and the angels sing blessings!

The joy of our "fancy new digs" had us floating around, happy to be home and settling in for another school year. Until.

All too often "until" enters the story, doesn't it? As we unpacked our boxes, something seemed a little bit off. Slowly it dawned on me that our boxes had been opened and rifled through by the workers who painted and installed the (still) glorious AC units. When I discovered opened packets of Jell-o, my suspicions were confirmed. Recalled now, years later, the scene is funny in my mind. Can you imagine you're a peasant from the Chinese countryside licking your finger, sticking it into the Jell-o powder and then in your mouth? In a land known for spicy food, cherry or lime flavor must have tasted awful.

But in that moment, humor escaped me. Instead, I felt the double-prong fork of violation and the lack of solid ground as a cross-cultural worker. Yes, this was *my* apartment, but it wasn't really. I couldn't even stay in my own home during the summer if I wanted to. And was it too much to ask that our boxes not be opened by strangers?! And if they must open them, was it too much to ask that they have the decency not to open our food?! As a typical American, the feeling that something must be done rose up in me (and Erin too). So, we did what you might expect: we went looking for answers.

To what? What questions could we really ask? What satisfying answers could have been given? All I can tell you is that the need to ask the questions and, to a certain extent, get a witness to the so-called injustice ran deep.

My teammate and I walked over to the FAO. Their office was on the second floor of an old dusty building. As we entered their office, Mr. Yao and Miss Luo sat at their respective desks facing each other. As tactfully as we could, we explained that during the summer our boxes had been gone through, some of the food opened, and a few of our belongings were missing. Mr. Yao, the head of the department, was a few years away from retirement and simply wanted to make it quietly to the days where he could spend hours in his rooftop garden. Instead, here he was having to navigate the murky waters of opened Jell-o packets.

At the end of the meeting, all of us were unsatisfied. We caused them to lose face by not letting the opened boxes simply be that .

.. opened boxes by curious peasants who had never been around actual foreigners or their things. We felt frustrated that our school officials hadn't really grasped the depth of the loss we felt. Instead of feeling validated, the incident had tapped into the reality of how far away the familiar was and how high the cost of Christ could be, even over small, silly parts of life.

If I could play that scene again, I wish that this final fruit of the Spirit had been more present in me that day. It's a mercy that "self-control" is not the first fruit listed. How different the tone of the fruit of the Spirit would be if Paul started the list with self-control and ended with love. Instead, he starts with love. When love is the heartbeat, self-control can take action. But without love? You end up in an office trying to seek justice over Jell-o. On the surface, we did exhibit self-control. We selected our words carefully. We tried not to be too accusatory. We followed cultural norms. As I said, if I could play that scene all over again, I might still have visited Mr. Yao and Miss Luo, but not on that day when my heart wanted justice and certainly not with the request for retribution that I knew, *I knew,* could go nowhere.

Prior to studying the fruit of the Spirit in preparation for this book, I thought of self-control in terms of three areas: my tone when I am angry, restraint when I want more, or making a wise choice in a tempting or difficult situation. While it's true that self-control is all of that, in the mystery and beauty of the Holy Spirit at work in us, that way of thinking merely scrapes the surface. The Greek word *egkrateia* can be translated as both self-control and self-mastery. *Egkrateia* is the virtue that makes a person such a master of themselves that they "are fit to be the servant of others."[35]

In the FAO with Mr. Yao and Miss Luo, was I fit to serve them? I can't say that I was.

NOVICE TO MASTER

I'm drawn to the idea of mastery because it holds space for both apprenticeship and growth. As an education major, part of my college program involved two student teaching assignments. On my first day of my first student teaching assignment, I drove to my assigned high school excited to finally, finally, finally be in a classroom, pouring knowledge and wisdom into students. (Clearly in need of a dose of humility!) Mr. Smith, not his real name, taught in the Social Studies Department and coached the football team. His student teaching experience had overwhelmed him, so in trying to spare me his pain, he had me sit for six weeks at a desk in the back of the classroom and watch him teach. Watching someone else do what I wanted to do without explaining what he was doing or preparing me to do it was not my dream come to life. I was glad when the experience came to an end because all I had mastered was the art of not looking bored in front of students for six hours a day.

My second student teaching assignment was at a junior high where I spent mornings in the math department with Mrs. Wolfe and afternoons in Mrs. Pent's social studies classroom. As in my first experience, I had a desk in the back of each room, but that is where the similarities stopped. For the first week, I watched in both classrooms but was invited to move around the classroom interacting and helping the students. Once I had my sea legs, the routine was to watch Mrs. Wolfe teach an algebra lesson in first period and then to teach the same lesson in her second period. For the first few weeks she stayed in the back of the room, serving as the "training wheels" for my learning, mostly silent but there to help if a question or situation came up that I didn't know how to navigate. As the weeks went by, our collective confidence in my teaching ability grew, and she'd sometimes leave the room for a few minutes. Slowly, the few minutes grew to the entire class period.

The same was true in the afternoons. Every spring Mrs. Pent taught a unit on George Orwell's classic *Animal Farm*. We'd review her lesson plans and look for opportunities for me to teach or even put my own spin on a lesson. I loved the collaborative nature of working with both of these master teachers, and to this day the thought of algebra or *Animal Farm* brings fond memories. I went on to teach math in that very school, and Mrs. Wolfe and Mrs. Pent—Judy and Cheryl—became my colleague.

In this parable of growth, which of the teachers was most like the Holy Spirit? While Mr. Smith thought he was protecting me by rarely letting me actually teach, he denied me the opportunity to experience freedom in the classroom. Instead, Mrs. Wolfe and Mrs. Pent embodied the role of the Holy Spirit in my life as they came alongside me. They equipped me with their experience, presence in the classroom, and friendship outside the classroom. They cheered me on, debriefed challenging encounters with me, and poured into me as a future teacher.

Mastery isn't a destination; it's a journey. Think of master bakers, master chefs, and master electricians, and even though they're experts in their fields, they haven't tapped out on growth. In His mercy and delight in you, God wants you to know both who He is and who you are. Not in a navel-gazing, "Do you know how lucky you are to know me?" vibe of a narcissist. But to give you the confidence of someone who knows that they're fiercely and wonderfully made.

Mastery also implies ownership and accountability. So, while self-control might focus on behavior—don't consume too much or too little, don't spend too much or too little, don't yell or withdraw—mastery goes deeper than behavior. I'm not saying that behavior doesn't matter; it does. But if you stop at behavior, you miss the richness of what lies below the surface in terms of motives, genetics, history, and personality.

You and I might have the same behavior that comes out of different motives or personal history. However, the more I understand myself, the more I can invite the Holy Spirit into an area of my life. So, what might be more like white-knuckling as I try to exhibit self-control becomes like a dance between me and the Holy Spirit. Just think of the areas for you and the Holy Spirit to explore through the lens of self-mastery:

— How you relate to your finances
— How you manage your relationship with time
— How you view and relate with authority
— How you determine which emotions are "good" and which are "bad"
— What pushes your justice button (and what doesn't)
— What healthy relationships look like with family members, friends, and strangers
— How you relate to and manage uncertainty
— What makes you feel secure, confident, or valuable
— What makes you feel insecure, unsure of yourself, or dismissed
— How you discern what God wants you to do in a situation
— How you handle someone or a situation you disagree with
— How you decide when and to whom you will submit
— How you live with or explain unanswered prayer

And the list goes on and on. The idea of self-mastery isn't limited to your own perception of your growth; it might be risky to ask, but how differently from you would your spouse, sibling, or teammate answer those questions? Or how would present-day you answer them differently than you did ten years ago? Two areas in which I've recently come to see myself in a richer light involve my sense of time and how I respond to various situations. Just now I had to laugh at myself because originally I wrote "how I respond to urgency." I had to switch the word "urgency" to "situations" for this very subject we are discussing! It's only in recent years, having grown in my self-awareness, that I realize I tend to view most situations as "urgent." I've consistently been the type of person who does my homework or work ahead of time . . . I don't like to wait till the last minute, because if something comes up last-minute, I like to have the margin to deal with it. Some of you reading this are nodding in understanding; others are shaking your heads, as doing something last-minute works better for you. (You are crazy people ☺.)

Here's an example of the internal tension that can arise from me being me: a family member mentions that they need my help with something, and I hear it as a request to drop everything and address their request immediately so that I don't have it hanging over my head. "Next time you're out, could you pick up some milk from the store?" Or "That cabinet hinge is broken; could you fix it when it's convenient?" Notice how the requests are phrased as nonurgent. But in my "don't leave anything to the last minute" wiring, they can feel falsely urgent. The more I've mastered myself with both this insight and the nudging from the Holy Spirit, the more I'm able to exhibit and experience the fruit of self-control. It's true that my initial reaction might be to want to drop everything and go to the store for the milk immediately. This might seem an inconsequential example of what self-control and self-mastery can look like, but this is exactly the kind of freedom Christ has for us. Freedom in the silly and the small parts of life and freedom for the large and extremely consequential parts of life.

During my pre-field orientation, each morning someone from the home office shared a devotion. Stacey, a beloved staff person who'd spent around three years on the field before returning to work in the home office, shared that "no matter where we were in the world, we were there." Most in the room had made a one-year commitment, so hearing from someone with the vantage point of having been on the field three years, it was almost like Moses had come down from a mountain. Stacey wanted to counterbalance the message that had been swirling around us for several months leading up to our departure. You know what I'm talking about. The pedestal that many cross-cultural workers are put on. "You're my hero!" and "I could never do what you're doing!" No matter how long you've been on the field, you know the truth of Stacey's core message: location does not magically make you holy.

I know that she was warning us to be honest about our sinful propensities. But what is equally true about taking your struggles to the field is that you also take your strengths. On an early morning video call with twelve other women serving cross-culturally, I asked each one to share something they're good at. Colleen shared that she's really good at doing laundry. There's no stain she can't get out, no load too intimidating. She loves, loves, loves doing laundry. Tina went next and told the group how, as the second youngest child in a large family, she didn't realize growing up that she had leadership skills. During her freshman year of college one of her friends said, "You're good at leading," and it was the first time she'd thought of herself as a leader. It was true, she is good at leading, and since then she's had the opportunity to use her leadership skills again and again. Melanie shared how she can connect easily with people not from her home culture. Jenn shared that as a teen her youth group leader was a nice older lady who had to step down and a young man took over the position. Instead of playing board games as they'd done with the nice lady, he introduced her to the wackier side of youth ministry. And she was hooked for life. It turns out she's good at connecting with teens. Sally shared how she's gifted at finding travel deals, which has benefited her family and others in her organization.

Person after person shared what she is good at. We talked about how self-mastery is a fruit of the Spirit and how part of the freedom we have in Christ is His desire for us to know what we're good at so it can continue to be developed. Prior to that conversation I'd never asked in a group for everyone to share what they are good at. Try it. Next time you're having dinner with a group, leading a team meeting, or looking for a conversation starter, ask people what they are good at.

With the women that morning, I pointed out something I hadn't noticed before: joy. Every single person smiled and had a bit more of a sparkle when she shared what she was good at. It didn't matter whether it was laundry, working with teens, leading large groups, or finding travel deals—the enjoyment couldn't be missed. This is why I want you to try it with your people! Like I did during the video call, you can then name the freedom and joy that God has for everyone, as He has for Melanie and Tina and each person in our group that day. Because it was a video call, they could see each other's faces and they knew I wasn't exaggerating: I was naming what we had all experienced. The sense of pride, competency, and fun was clear to all.

Too often I have been a "novice of myself" instead of a master. Take time with God to work through the list above and other tools that allow you to know yourself better as a part of the fruit of self-mastery fully developing in you.

THE ROLE OF LIMITS

Talking about self-mastery also involves self-control. Now that we've explored the freedom and joy that comes from self-mastery, we also need to explore the idea of limits and maturity. While you're freed up from the pressure of being good at everything, the flip side is that you are also limited and can't have or be everything. Peter Scazzero has been instrumental in helping many of his readers understand that limits allow them to acknowledge their humanity. In addition, when we bump into our limits, it's a chance to remember that we are not God. This is both freeing and frustrating! "Limits are behind all loss. We cannot do or be anything [or have the housing] we want. God has placed enormous limits around even the most gifted of us. Why? To keep us grounded, to keep us humble. . . . Our culture routinely interprets losses as alien invasions that interrupt our 'normal' lives. We numb our pain through denial, blaming, rationalization, addictions, and avoidance. We search for spiritual shortcuts around our wounds. We demand others take away our pain."[36]

Let's talk about how different the reality of life and ministry on the field is compared to what you thought it would be like. I don't know about your life, but my life looked a bit more like mundane daily life than thousands lining up to be baptized. And the pace?! My life often existed in extremes: either life was moving at the pace of molasses and I was painfully aware of hours of boredom, or it felt like I was on a roller coaster that slowed, fooling me into thinking the ride was over only to pick up speed again upon a descent. I once sat down to figure out how much money supporters had given in my name over the years, and the amount about made me sick. When I looked at what I had "accomplished" compared to the dollar amount donated, I felt like a huckster.

This is why we need ongoing conversations about limits, self-mastery, and maturity. These conversations are vital for fruitfulness because faulty thinking can sneak in so easily. We're slowing down to take the time to let the idea of limits soak into our souls. We're limited—and prepare to cringe with me—by what Scazzero describes as our "enormous" limits. Though even now as I write this part of me resists this truth, another part of me nods a knowing "It's true, you are limited. You're enormously limited, Amy."

God mysteriously enlarges your soul through the work of grieving and growing into your limits. Sometimes the growing is in a relatively small area. In a conversation with Ken and his wife who were on a sabbatical from their work in Africa, he mentioned how this season off the field is different from previous ones because of apps that make communication readily available. As an area director, during previous times away from the field he was able to limit communication with those on the field to occasional emails; however, this time with the proliferation of apps that make communication handy, it's been difficult to rest because of the daily messages he receives from one person or another. You're probably nodding in understanding because most of us, myself included, have apps that are "mixed." If the app was only used for ministry, he could simply delete it or change his settings while he's on sabbatical. Instead, "mixed" apps are used for both personal and work/ministry. So, if he were to delete the app, it's also where his siblings have a group chat, and he'd miss out on family connections. Since deleting the app isn't a viable option, we talked about what he *could* do. In his case, most of what he's being messaged about is important but not urgent, so he's going to pick one day of the week and let his colleagues know that he'll respond to them on that day.

For Ken, growing in understanding limits involves limiting work, probably something we can all relate to, as boundaries between being "on" and "off" can be muddied by our smart devices. But what about a limit that has been imposed upon you? A limit you may not want. Maybe the country you feel called to serve will not grant you a visa. Or you're struggling with something personal like primary or secondary infertility, the death of a spouse, children facing challenges that feel insurmountable, an apartment that feels too small for the number of bodies living in it, or a desire to be married? Of course, you could see miraculous change in any of them, but there's also a good chance you may not. In her book *This Too Shall Last*, K.J. Ramsey explores the topic of finding grace when suffering lasts, or, to put it another way, finding grace when a limit has been placed where we don't want one. I love how she points us to a deeper understanding of what true transformation is in light of limits we don't want:

A common bit of advice we get in suffering is to think more about others, to get our minds off ourselves. We are transformed not by thinking less about ourselves but by thinking differently about ourselves. Transformation happens in paying attention to our lives with kindness and compassion rooted in the care of a God who so loved us that he died for us. We are often taught holiness involves thinking less about ourselves and more about Jesus.

We need Jesus—oh, how we need Jesus!—but we need him in the substance of our lives, in the emotional floods and deserts, in the places where we feel abandoned, overwhelmed, and lifeless. Believing you need to think less about yourself may be leading you farther away from experiencing the presence of God refashioning you into the likeness of Christ. By judging our lives instead of inhabiting them, we miss dwelling in the place where God silently clothes us in his redeeming love.[37]

I don't want to minimize the pain of limits that show up in the form of missing out on holidays and family gatherings on the other side of the world, not being allowed to serve where we want to, or dealing with chronic pain. The fruit of self-control isn't about learning to make the most of our limits. It's not about relishing the ways we need to control ourselves. But as K.J. Ramsey suggests, we should also not miss out on dwelling with God in these limits. When we're so focused on escaping our limits or managing them, we miss the actual living that can go on within them.

SELF-CONTROL IN UNLIKELY PLACES

In the chapter on faithfulness we looked at how part of yourself tries to protect your soul by acting like a manager who ends up meddling more than helping. As you mature in walking with the Spirit, you're able to be faithful without having to meddle. When we discussed gentleness, we looked at how your soul protector might confuse gentleness with not engaging. As you mature in this fruit, you'll be able to be more present in a situation without having to lash out or withdraw. We come now to our final soul protector who, in this case, thinks they are helping you by acting like a firefighter. At their worst, firefighters don't trust true self-control to get the job done, so they're ready to swoop in and often make a situation worse in the aftermath.[38]

John 15 is often quoted as a picture of abiding in Christ and rightly so—but what if it is also a picture of this final fruit? Jesus said, "I am the true vine, and my Father is the gardener. He cuts off every branch in me that bears no fruit, while every branch that does bear fruit he prunes so that it will be even more fruitful" (John 15:1–2). We all experience seasons where roles, relationships, even dreams have either died or need to be pruned. It's tempting to wonder what went wrong. Was this death or pruning avoidable? But that might not be the most helpful question. In this section of John, Jesus is preparing the disciples for His absence. Self-control and self-mastery can be misleading because it can sound like it is all up to us and our will power. So, when something dies or has gotten a bit out of control, is it the fault of the vine? No. We're back to walking with the Spirit or abiding in Christ being more like a dance than a math formula.

When it comes to the fruit of self-mastery and this passage in John, we need to be open to the truth of seasonality. At times we need to let the dead be cut out and other times the out-of-control be pruned to create space for further growth.

As I mentioned earlier in this chapter, mastery isn't a destination but a journey. Combined with faithfulness and gentleness, this final inward-focused fruit is one for the long haul. Years after my encounter with the FAO and the opened Jell-o packets, I traveled to Tibet to visit fellow teachers in my organization. In my hotel room I took off a necklace that was given to me by a dear friend and set in on the desk. The next few days were full with meetings, meals, and quality time with my TIC colleagues. A couple of nights into my visit, when I got back to my hotel room, something seemed a bit out of place, but I couldn't put my finger on what. And then I had the sinking feeling that the necklace was gone.

I searched everywhere, like the woman searching for her coin in Luke 15, but couldn't find it. To directly accuse someone of stealing is very serious and in Asia can lead to such loss of face that the truth won't come out. I thought and prayed about how to respond. The next morning I went to the front desk and explained that my necklace was missing and I had looked and couldn't find it. Thankfully, I had grown in my understanding of the culture and of myself. I paused, "If the girl who cleaned my room happened to find it, I'd be very, very happy."

The young woman working the front desk opened her eyes wider and wider as she nodded, understanding my meaning without anyone losing face and the s-word (stolen) never being said. Walking out of the office, I enjoyed the feeling that I'd finally, after many years, figured out how to do something indirectly. Opening the door that evening, I didn't know what I'd find. I turned on the light and walked toward the desk, and guess what? There in all its glory was my necklace.

The next morning, when I checked out at the front desk, I left a tip for the girl who found it—as yet another indirect gesture, this time to find out if she had been fired. The same woman from the day before was working the front desk, and she asked me if it was the short or fat girl who cleaned my room, indirectly indicating that both were still employed. What a relief that I hadn't cost someone her job! As horrible as the feeling of losing control can be, all the more so is the joy of the fruit of self-control, especially when it also reflects self-mastery.

In the book of Mark, Jesus healed a blind man by spitting in his eyes (Mark 8:23). It fascinates me that Jesus asked the man, "Do you see anything?" Did Jesus need feedback on how well He'd performed a miracle? No. Yet the man unexpectedly answered, "I see people; they look like trees walking around" (Mark 8:24). Jesus put his hands on the man's eyes for a second time, and then the man "saw everything clearly" (Mark 8:25). To a certain extent we're all blind to ourselves, but God wants us to see ourselves clearly—the good, the bad, and the broken. So that we can be grateful for and enjoy the good. In addition, we can heal, grow, and confess and turn from the bad and broken parts of ourselves. We might think that taking selfies is something new. But God's been interested in the inward growth of faithfulness, gentleness, and self-control long before cameras were invented. God's love goes beyond the surface of a selfie or the capturing of a moment all the way to the depths of our souls and the freedom He has for us there.

LET US PRAY

Grant me, O Lord, for your sake, through the work of your Holy Spirit, love for those I've come to serve and those I serve with, joy in the midst of the mundane and the miraculous of my life, and peace that starts within me and flows to others.

Add to these fruit that flow from You patience, that I may be long-tempered with those I interact with today, kindness that is useful to them and life-giving to me, and goodness that moves me to action.

Help me to be consistently moving toward the person you want me to be as I am faithful in word and deed, to exhibit gentleness that is always angry at the right time and never angry at the wrong time, and to be able to master myself in such a way that points to you, O Lord. Amen.

CONCLUSION

I n the introduction I made an observation and wondered, is burnout on the field related to being more focused on ministry fruitfulness than on personal fruitfulness?

What's ironic about ministry fruitfulness is that every organization will have its own definition of "fruitfulness" on the field. Though there isn't a universal definition, as I've discussed this topic with people in different organizations, every organization, without exception, has one. I have yet to find an organization that doesn't have either a spoken or an unspoken way of communicating what it considers fruitful. Also, almost without exception, these metrics can slip into a modern version of returning to the law.

In TIC, we said that the work was the Lord's, and I know that the leaders truly believed that. But it was often a mixed message because of the way "the work of the Lord" was shared. When we'd gather for an organization-wide conference, time was usually slotted for a few testimonies. I'll never forget the year that Ken and Barbie (not their real names) were asked to share about a typical week. On top of a full teaching load for both of them, they shared how on Monday nights they had a Bible study, on Tuesday nights Ken discipled a group of guys and Barbie discipled a group of women, on Wednesday nights they had another Bible study for campus leaders, and on and on it went. Six nights out of the week their schedule was filled to the brim with ministry. Instead of being encouraged at what God was doing, most of us in that room felt like slackers. Since Ken and Barbie were selected to share their story, didn't that mean theirs was the kind of behavior and focus that the organization truly valued? Was that what fruitfulness looked like? You can imagine the hushed conversations in the hallways and lines for meals after they spoke. "Is this what TIC expects of all of us? Was that an indirect message?" It was rare to have a testimony from a "normal" situation that mirrored the majority of our lives. While the hoped-for message was "Look what God is doing!" often the indirect message was, "And this could be your story, too, if you worked harder."

As I said, I know that TIC's leadership truly believes that the work is the Lord's . . . *and* . . . A subtle "and" seemed ever present. Oftentimes "ands" are good, but not here. This "and" leads straight back to the law.

I've proposed a different vision for us in this book. What would it look like for an organization to define true fruitfulness as freedom in Christ that is rooted in reality and experienced with God, others, and yourself? That's what I've envisioned for us in this book. It's not flashy, but it is life-giving, and the only way to experience the true freedom that Paul described to the Galatians is through Christ. This type of fruitfulness is available to you right now whether or not you're with an organization. Whether or not your organization is willing to do the hard work to move away from the subtle "ands" that can sneak into its messages and, really, into all of our thinking. Whether or not others join you on this journey.

Metrics aren't the core problem. Every organization, team, and individual can benefit from standards and measures. But I'm hoping and praying and trusting that as more and more of us taste this type of fruitfulness, we'll find ourselves surrounded by others who are also measuring their fruitfulness first by love, joy,

    peace,

        patience,

            kindness,

                goodness,

                    gentleness,

                        faithfulness,

and self-control . . . as we walk and work with the Holy Spirit all the days of our lives.

"Against such things there is no law. Those who belong to Christ Jesus have crucified the flesh with its passions and desires. Since we live by the Spirit, let us keep in step with the Spirit. Let us not become conceited, provoking and envying each other" (Galatians 5:23–26).

ONE LAST TIME, LET'S PRAY:

Grant me, O Lord, for your sake, through the work of your Holy Spirit, love for those I've come to serve and those I serve with, joy in the midst of the mundane and the miraculous of my life, and peace that starts within me and flows to others.

Add to these fruit that flow from You patience, that I may be long-tempered with those I interact with today, kindness that is useful to them and life-giving to me, and goodness that moves me to action.

Help me to be consistently moving toward the person you want me to be as I am faithful in word and deed, to exhibit gentleness that is always angry at the right time and never angry at the wrong time, and to be able to master myself in such a way that points to you, O Lord. Amen.

ACKNOWLEDGMENTS

As any author will tell you, though the writer's name is the one on the cover, no book is written without a community. This particular book was born out of my research for *Connected*. The more I learned about the fruit of the Spirit, the more I wanted everyone to know what I was learning! It didn't matter what I was invited to speak on, what podcast I was a guest on, or whether you were interested or not . . . I talked about the fruit of the Spirit! So, first I want to thank all of you who put up with me as I worked on this book.

Every book I write has a couple of vivid memories associated with it. When I think of *Becoming More Fruitful*, I am instantly back on the couch in a townhouse in the mountains of Colorado. It was spring break and friends were off skiing while I stayed back and worked on this book. I turned on the TV to check on my beloved Kansas Jayhawks in the Big 12 tournament. This was March of 2020 and though you know what's coming, I did not. I was shocked that the Jayhawks had pulled out of the tournament, which meant they would not go to the NCAA tournament. I texted my friends as they skied. I couldn't think clearly and put away the chapter I was working on.

Even though this book has nothing directly to do with the Covid-19 pandemic or all the disruptions we experienced, I cannot avoid acknowledging that season and the way it indirectly shows up here. The pandemic slowed down the writing process, and it allowed me to live out walking with the Spirit in a real-life laboratory. I'm grateful for the Writers on the Rock community as we all leaned into each other as writers as the months unfolded. Thank you. In addition, thank you to the KB Mastermind Group; we might be small, but our hour-long Skype calls every two weeks do more to keep me accountable to my goals than anything else I do. Britta Lafont, Esther Wodrich, and Kathy Strong, I love you and a million thanks.

I continue to marvel at the editing process and how it parallels the role of the Holy Spirit. Good editors are invested in a book, and I am fortunate to have such an editor. Deb Hall, my beloved editor, once again, I cannot imagine what my writing would be like without you. You are kind, encouraging, but no mere cheerleader, you pointed out where I was not clear, where I was a bit over the edge on snark, and where an example was not, in fact, an example. I have learned more about grammar and clarity in writing from you than from anyone else. Your editing talents are legendary in Colorado. I also highly recommend Deb's editing to you, dear reader. You can reach her at The Write Insight: http://thewriteinsight.com. Also, I hope you do judge this book by its fantastic cover because Vanessa Mendozzi is a design genius. She can take a few vague ideas I have for a cover and then create a cover that is stunning. Vanessa also did the interior design of the book. She is fast, affordable, and so easy to work with! Contact Vanessa at https://www.vanessamendozzidesign.com. Thank you, Amy Boucher Pye, for offering your expert eye to the copy on the back cover!

I am grateful for my family. I love you, Mom, Dad, Elizabeth, Laura, Del, Sue, Emily, Katy, Anna, and Chloe.

ABOUT THE AUTHOR

A my Young is a writer, speaker, and advocate for embracing the messy middle in life. She lived in China for nearly twenty years. As a cofounder of the digital community Velvet Ashes, Amy was on the cutting edge of using technology to support and develop cross-cultural workers. She founded Global Trellis an online space for personal, professional, and spiritual development of cross-cultural workers. Amy enjoys cheering for the Denver Broncos, the Kansas Jayhawks, and libraries. Though she misses steaming dumplings in Beijing, Amy currently lives in Denver, Colorado and, much to her surprise, enjoys gardening.

ALSO BY AMY YOUNG

Looming Transitions:
Starting and Finishing Well in Cross-Cultural Service

Looming Transitions:
Twenty-Two Activities for Families in Transition
Looming Transitions Workbook

Love, Amy:
An Accidental Memoir Told in Newsletters from China

Enjoying Newsletters:
How to Write Christian Communications People Want to Read

Getting Started:
Making the Most of Your First Year in Cross-Cultural Service

Connected:
Starting Your Overseas Life Spiritually Fed

ENDNOTES

1. "Debaucheries," Dictionary.com, https://www.dictionary.com/browse/debauchery.
2. *The Expositor's Bible Commentary*, vol. 10 (Grand Rapids, MI: Zondervan, 1976), 498.
3. *The Expositor's Bible Commentary*, 498.
4. "Team Factors," The MissionsExperience.com, January 25, 2020, https://themissionsexperience.weebly.com/blog/team-factors.
5. C.S. Lewis, *The Four Loves* (New York: Harper Collins, 1960).
6. Sarah Ruden, *Paul Among the People: The Apostle Reinterpreted and Reimagined in His Own Time* (New York: Random House Inc, 2011), 181.
7. Ruden, *Paul Among the People*, 180.
8. Greg McKeown, *Effortless: Make It Easier to Do What Matters Most* (New York: Random House, 2021), 56.
9. Justin Alfred, "Biblical Hebrew Applied: Psalm 23 (Part 2)," The BLB Blog, April 11, 2012, https://blogs.blueletterbible.org/blb/2012/04/11/biblical-hebrew-applied-psalm-23-part-2/.
10. Doug Hershey, "The True Meaning of Shalom," *FIRM Israel*, January 3, 2020, https://firmisrael.org/learn/the-meaning-of-shalom/.
11. Later I found out that I was the fifth woman in leadership he'd had troubles with. But in that moment, I felt like I was in survival mode for my job and my reputation within the organization. As "good Christian women" the other women either hadn't said

anything or weren't taken seriously and didn't push the issue. Instead, the organization deemed the VP's role to be vital to our mission; his bad behavior was excused and we lost capable leaders. Thankfully, I was one of the last women he treated this way and wouldn't let the issue be swept under the rug. It took a few years, but he is no longer with TIC.

12. Jamie Good, "Struggling Vines Produce Better Wines," Wineanorak.com, http://www.wineanorak.com/struggle.htm.

13. William Barclay, *The Letters to the Galatians and Ephesians* (Philadelphia: Westminster Press, 1976), 55.

14. "3115. makrothumia," *Strong's Greek*, Biblehub.com, https://biblehub.com/greek/3115.htm.

15. "5544. chréstotés," *Strong's Greek*, Biblehub.com, https://biblehub.com/greek/5544.htm.

16. "Struggling Vines Produce Better Wines," Wineanorak.com, https://wineanorak.com/struggle.htm.

17. "Random Act of Kindness," *Grammarist*, https://Grammarist.com/, December 7, 2017, https://grammarist.com/phrase/random-act-of-kindness/.

18. "The History of *Random Acts of Kindness*," Random Acts of Kindness, https://Makeadiff.wordpress.com/, June 2, 2006, https://makeadiff.wordpress.com/2006/06/02/the-history-of-random-acts-of-kindness/.

19. "Movie Day at the Supreme Court or 'I Know It When I See It': A History of the Definition of Obscenity," FindLaw, https://Corporate.findlaw.com, April 26, 2016, https://corporate.findlaw.com/litigation-disputes/movie-day-at-the-supreme-court-or-i-know-it-when-i-see-it-a.html.

20. *The Expositor's Bible Commentary*, vol. 10 (Grand Rapids, MI: Zondervan, 1976), 499.

21. Maggie, "Types of Attachment: Fostering a Secure Attachment in Your Baby," Blog.kinedu.com, September 28, 2016, https://blog.kinedu.com/

types-of-attachment-fostering-a-secure-attachment-in-your-baby/.

22. Alison Cook and Kimberly Miller, *Boundaries for Your Soul: How to Turn Your Overwhelming Thoughts and Feelings into Your Greatest Allies* (Nashville: Nelson Books, 2018), 31.

23. Cook and Miller, *Boundaries for Your Soul*, 32.

24. Cook and Miller, *Boundaries for Your Soul*, 33.

25. Cook and Miller, *Boundaries for Your Soul*, 33.

26. Henri Nouwen, *Can You Drink the Cup?* (Notre Dame, IN: Ave Maria Press, 1996), 63–64.

27. Nouwen, Can You Drink the Cup?, 63–64.

28. Amy Young, "I Want to Blame China, but They Are My Elbows," The Messy Middle, February 1, 2013, https://www.messymiddle.com/i-want-to-blame-china-but-they-are-my-elbows/.

29. I've hunted high and low on the internet and cannot find this article. I'm sorry, author and publisher, that I cannot give you the proper credit you deserve!

30. William Barclay, *The Letters to the Galatians and Ephesians* (Philadelphia: West Minster Press, 1970), 56–57.

31. *The Expositor's Bible Commentary*, vol. 10 (Grand Rapids, MI: Zondervan, 1976), 499.

32. Alison Cook and Kimberly Miller, *Boundaries for Your Soul: How to Turn Your Overwhelming Thoughts and Feelings into Your Greatest Allies* (Nashville: Nelson Books, 2018), 35.

33. Joann Pittman, "Nothing Is as It Seems," JoannPittman.com, November 8, 2011, https://joannpittman.com/chinese-society/2011/nothing-is-as-it-seems/.

34. Rob Gifford, *China Road: A Journey into the Future of a Rising Power* (New York: Random House, 2007), 274.

35. William Barclay, *Letters to the Galatians and Ephesians* (Philadelphia: West Minster Press, 1970), 57.

36. Peter Scazzero, *Emotionally Healthy Spirituality: Unleash a Revolution in Your Life in Christ* (Grand Rapids, MI: Zondervan,

2006), chapter 7.

37. K.J. Ramsey, *This Too Shall Last: Finding Grace When Suffering Lingers* (Grand Rapids, MI: Zondervan 2020), 110.

38. Alison Cook and Kimberly Miller, *Boundaries for Your Soul: How to Turn Your Overwhelming Thoughts and Feelings into Your Greatest Allies* (Nashville: Nelson Books, 2018), 34.